POST ROAD

SUBMISSION AND SUBSCRIPTION INFORMATION

Post Road publishes twice yearly and accepts submissions in all genres.

• POETRY: Electronic submissions at poetry@postroadmag.com.
*Microsoft Word documents as attachments only. All other formats or submission of work
in the body of an email cannot be considered.*

• NONFICTION: Editor, Post Road, 203 Bedford Ave., Brooklyn, NY 11211

• ALL OTHER SUBMISSIONS should be addressed to the section editor and sent to:
P.O. Box 590663, Newton Center, MA 02459

• ADMINISTRATIVE: Post Road, 853 Broadway, Suite 1516, Box 85, New York, NY   10003

Subscriptions: Individuals, $16/year; Institutions, $32/year;
outside the U.S. please add $6/year for postage.

Distributed by:

Bernhard DeBoer, Inc., Nutley, N.J.

Ingram Periodicals Inc., LaVergne, TN

PRINTED IN CANADA

website: www.postroadmag.com

POST ROAD

Founding Editors
Jaime Clarke
David Ryan

Managing Editor
Catherine Parnell

Art Editor
Susan Breen

Criticism Editor
Hillary Chute

Etcetera Editors
Jaime Clarke
Alden Jones

Fiction Editors
Rebecca Boyd
Michael Rosovsky
David Ryan

Nonfiction Editors
Pete Hausler
Marcus McGraw

Poetry Editors
Mark Conway
Anne McCarty

Associate Poetry Editor: Jeffrey Shotts

Recommendations Editor
Tim Huggins

Theatre Editor
David Ryan

Web Editor
Ricco Villanueva Siasoco

Web Designer
Sean Dessureau

Copy Editor
Heather E. Fisher

Layout and Design
Josephine Bergin

Special thanks to:

Jennifer Chunias
Sandy Fine
Kyle Hofmann

Kelsey Lemaster
Randi Triant

We would like to thank our patrons for their generous support:

Steve Banker and Nancy Simpson-Banker
Amy Bull Burke and Paul W. Burke
JoeAnn Hart
Susan S. Jones

Marie Claire Leng
Jane A. Little
Nicole C. Newton
Oscar and Penelope Sanders

Table of Contents

6 Contributor Notes

Poetry

11 A Confederacy + Mr. Sweatner's Parade *David Daniel*

13 The Nineteenth-Century Novel + The Nineteenth-Century Novel II *Eve Grubin*

15 A Hunger So Honed + Self Portrait as the Letter Y *Tracy K. Smith*

20 The Lais of Lost Long Days + Stripped from the Waist Up, Love *Olena Kalytiak Davis*

24 Cellist + Dogs Resembling Their Owner *Peter Jay Shippy*

26 Three Months, No Kidding + Salt *Alison Stine*

Nonfiction

31 Sea Monsters *Kate Crane*

39 The Middle-Aged Man and the Sea *Larry O'Connor*

48 Third Street. Stambaugh, Michigan: Late Spring, 1972 *Chad Faries*

52 City Storms *Jeffrey M. Bockman*

Criticism

57 On the Aesthetic Agenda of the Antiwar Movement *Lori Cole*

Art

66 Mary Armstrong: Paintings *Introduction by Claude Cernuschi*

73 Stoney Conley: Paintings *Introduction by Claude Cernuschi*

Fiction

83 Dream Children *Edith Pearlman*

89 Since It's You *Peter Brown*

100 What We Do *Mat Johnston*

114 Untitled as of Yet *Sarah Nankin*

116 Activist *Andrew Richmond*

Theatre

121 Note to *Post Road* Readers *Jonathan Ames*

Recommendations

129 *Middlemarch* by George Eliot *Donna Morrissey*

131 *The Savage Girl* by Alex Shakar *Henry Presente*

134 *Italian Days* by Barbara Grizzuti Harrison *Karl Iagnemma*

136 *Plant Life* by Pamela Duncan *Lynn Pruett*

138 *Antarctica* by Claire Keegan *Michael Lowenthal*

140 Robert Walser *Kevin Canty*

142 *Open Doors* by Leonardo Sciascia *Peter Orner*

143 Michael Byers and *The Coast of Good Intentions* *Roy Parvin*

145 *True Grit* by Charles Portis *Tom Franklin*

146 Three Australian Novelists *Sabina Murray*

Etcetera

151 Index: *Lolita* A-Z

169 Interview: April Bernard *Reb Livingston*

183 Reprint: Henry James on Turgenev

Contributor Notes

Jonathan Ames is the author of *I Pass Like Night, The Extra Man, What's Not to Love?*, and *My Less Than Secret Life*. His latest novel, *Wake Up, Sir!*, is due out from Scribner in 2004. He is the winner of a Guggenheim Fellowship and teaches at Columbia University. His one-man show *Oedipussy* debuted off-off-Broadway, and his record as an amateur boxer, fighting under the nickname "The Herring Wonder," is 0-1.

Mary Armstrong: I had a very good upbringing for a painter. I grew up on a small farm far from town. My mother died when I was five years old. My father, a teacher, farmer, and writer, raised my brothers and I. There was ample space and abundant solitude in my childhood for the growth of a very rich fantasy life deeply connected to nature and for the development of a fiercely independent spirit.

Jeffrey M. Bockman has published short stories and creative non-fiction in various print and digital literary journals, such as *Chelsea, CrossConnect, The Connecticut Review* and *The Iowa Review Web*. With Jenine Gordon, he co-founded the magazine *Literal Latté*, which they published in sin together for a number of years before marrying. He has an M.A. in Creative Writing from NYU and a Ph.D. in the sciences from Berkeley.

Peter Brown is at work on his first novel, *The Dwarf of Teheran*, and a collection of stories called *Since It's You*. His work has appeared in *Salamander*, where he is currently editor-at-large, and in *the new renaissance*. He is also a visual artist. Some of his drawings can be viewed at www.economics.harvard.edu/~pbrown/drawings.html.

Kevin Canty has written the novels *Into the Great Wide Open* and *Nine Below Zero*, as well as the story collections *A Stranger in This World* and *Honeymoon*. His essays and stories have appeared in *The New Yorker, Esquire, GQ, Vogue*, and elsewhere. He lives and writes, among other things, in Missoula, Montana, where he teaches in the MFA program at the University of Montana and plays slide guitar in the Pleasure Kings.

Claude Cernuschi received his MA and PhD from the Institute of Fine Arts, New York University, and is presently associate professor of art history at Boston College. He is the author of *Jackson Pollock: Meaning and Significance, Jackson Pollock: "Psychoanalytic" Drawings, Not an Illustration, But the Equivalent: A Cognitive Approach to Abstract Expressionism*, and *Re/Casting Kokoschka: Ethics and Aesthetics, Epistemology and Politics in Fin-de-Siecle Vienna*.

Lori Cole was a 2002-3 Helena Rubinstein Critical Studies Fellow of the Whitney Museum of American Art Independent Study Program. She has contributed articles to the *Providence Phoenix* and the *Village Voice* and currently lives in Brooklyn.

Stoney Conley received fellowships from the Ballinglen Arts Foundation in Ireland and the Fine Arts Work Center in Provincetown. He has received an NEA and the Fulbright Hayes Grant to Italy. Italian culture and Irish heritage have been the North Star and compass, a guide for his creative work. He is also a teacher and curator.

Kate Crane grew up in the city that reads (and breeds, and bleeds): Baltimore, MD. For the past eight years, she has lived in Brooklyn, NY, where she is a writer and activist with Reclaim the Streets and other global justice groups. Recently, her work has appeared in *New York Press, World War 3 Illustrated*, and *Left Turn*.

David Daniel is the poetry editor of *Ploughshares* and a songwriter. His book, *Seven-Star Bird*, is forthcoming any day now from Graywolf Press. He will be touring the country promoting both the book and a CD for most of 2004.

Olena Kalytiak Davis is the author of *And Her Soul Out of Nothing* (University of Wisconsin, 1997) and *Shattered Sonnets Love Cards and Other Off and Back Handed Importunities*, which will be out this fall from Tin House/Bloomsbury. She lives and sighs in Anchorage, Alaska.

Chad Faries grew up in the Upper Peninsula of Michigan. He holds a PhD from the University of Wisconsin-Milwaukee and is contributing editor for *The Cream City Review*. He has published interviews, essays, poems, and photographs in *Exquisite Corpse*, *New American Writing*, *Afterimage*, *Phoebe*, *Prosodia*, *Mudfish*, *Barrow Street*, *Oxford Magazine*, *Left Curve*, *Yefief*, and others. His manuscript *Measuring Clouds with a Stick* was a finalist for the 2000 Academy of American Poets Walt Whitman Award. Currently, he is a Fulbright Fellow in Budapest, Hungary, where he teaches at Eötvös Loránd University (ELTE).

Tom Franklin is the author of the highly acclaimed collection, *Poachers* (William Morrow), named by *Esquire* as a Distinguished First Book of Fiction for 1999. The title story from *Poachers* won the 1999 Edgar Allan Poe Award for Best Mystery Story. His novel, *Hell at the Breech* (William Morrow), was published in May of 2003. He lives in Oxford, Mississippi, with his wife, the poet Beth Ann Fennelly, and their daughter, Claire Elizabeth.

Eve Grubin's poems have appeared or are forthcoming in *Barrow Street*, *LIT*, *The Drunken Boat*, and elsewhere. She is the Programs Director at the Poetry Society of America, and she teaches at The New School.

Karl Iagnemma's short stories have won the *Playboy* college fiction contest and *The Paris Review* Discovery Prize, and have been selected for *The Best American Short Stories* and *Pushcart Prize* anthologies. His writing has appeared in *Tin House* and *Zoetrope*, among other publications. His first collection of stories, *On the Nature of Human Romantic Interaction*, was published in April by the Dial Press. He is currently a research scientist in the mechanical engineering department at the Massachusetts Institute of Technology, specializing in robotics.

Mat Johnston was born in Fergus Falls, Minnesota, in 1980. In 2003 he received a BA from Sarah Lawrence College. He lives temporarily in Brooklyn.

Reb Livingston is a poet and jewelry designer living in Reston, VA. Her work has appeared in *5AM*, *LIT*, *Slope*, and *Drunken Boat*. Visit her website: www.reblivingston.net.

Michael Lowenthal is the author of the novels *Avoidance* (Graywolf Press, 2002) and *The Same Embrace* (Dutton, 1998). He lives in Boston.

Donna Morrissey is the author of the novel, *Kit's Law* (Houghton Mifflin), winner of the 2000 Canadian Booksellers Association Libris Award and the British Winifred Holtby Prize, as well as most recently *Downhill Change* (Houghton Mifflin). Born and raised in Newfoundland, Morrissey now lives in Halifax, Nova Scotia.

Sabina Murray was born in 1968 and grew up in Australia and the Philippines. She is the author of the collection *The Caprices* (Houghton Mifflin) and the novel *Slow Burn*. Her stories have appeared in *Ploughshares*, *Ontario Review*, *New England Review*, and other magazines. Her screenplay, *Beautiful Country*, goes into production this October with Hans Moland directing, Terry Malick producing, and Nick Nolte and Harvey Keitel in major roles. She is a former Bunting Fellow at Harvard University and a recipient of a major grant from the Massachusetts Cultural Council. Murray is currently the Writer-in-Residence at Phillips Academy Andover.

Sarah Nankin attends New School University. She lives in Brooklyn, NY.

Larry O'Connor is a journalist and writer whose memoir, *Tip of the Iceberg*, was published in 2002 by the University of Georgia Press. His articles have appeared in *The New York Times* and *The Globe and Mail*, and his commentaries have been heard on National Public Radio. An essay entitled "My Belt" was published in 1988 by St. Martin's Press in an anthology, *A Few Thousand Words About Love*. He is co-editor with his wife, Mary Morris, of *Maiden Voyages*. Larry O'Connor edits overseas editions of *The Wall Street Journal* and lives in Brooklyn with his wife and daughter.

Peter Orner is the author of *Esther Stories*, a finalist for the Hemingway Foundation/PEN Award and winner of the Prix de Rome from the American Academy of Arts and Letters. His work has appeared in *The Atlantic Monthly* and *The Best American Stories* and been awarded a Pushcart Prize. He lives in Rome.

Roy Parvin is the author of *The Loneliest Road in America* (Chronicle Books), a collection of short stories, and *In the Snow Forest* (W.W. Norton), a book of novellas. His fiction has been awarded the Katherine Anne Porter Prize and included in *The Best American Short Stories*. He lives in the woods of northern California with his wife, Janet, and two border collies and a cat. Rumors that his next book will be a novel are entirely true.

Edith Pearlman's short stories have appeared in many prize anthologies: the *O. Henry Prize Collection, The Best American Short Stories, Pushcart Press, Best Stories from the South*, and others. Her own first collection, *Vaquita*, was published in 1996. It won the Drue Heinz award for fiction. Her second, *Love Among the Greats*, was published in November 2002. It won the Spokane Prize for Fiction.

Henry Presente whiles away his daylight hours working in the business development and marketing department of a public affairs firm. A graduate of the journalism program at the George Washington University in DC, he haunts that city's streets, feeding an incessant desire to keep up with current events, as well as an appetite for empanadas. His work has been published in *EWG Presents*.

Lynn Pruett is a graduate of Mount Holyoke College and the University of Alabama, where she received her MFA. She has been published in *American Voice, Southern Exposure, Black Warrior Review*, and *Telling Stories*, an anthology. She is the author of the debut novel, *Ruby River* (Atlantic Monthly Press).

Andrew Richmond was raised in Missouri. He has lived in Scotland, Georgia and Wisconsin and currently lives and works in New York.

Peter Jay Shippy's book *Thieves' Latin* won the 2002 Iowa Poetry Prize. He received a writing fellowship from the NEA for 2003. His poetry and fiction can be read in *Denver Quarterly, Boston Review*, and *boomerangUK.com*.

Tracy K. Smith lives in Brooklyn, NY. Her first collection of poems, *The Body's Question*, won the 2002 Cave Canem Poetry Prize, selected by Kevin Young, and will be published in October 2003 by Graywolf Press.

Alison Stine is the author of *Lot of my Sister* (Kent State University Press, 2001). She has poems forthcoming in *Poetry* and *Salt Hill*. Her work has also appeared in *The Paris Review, Kenyon Review, Mid-American Review*, and *Black Warrior Review*, among others. She lives with a piano and a cat named Easter in an apartment she would like to paint red.

POETRY

POST ROAD

A Confederacy

David Daniel

A butcher bird sings by the flooded Nigger Flat
Along the shore of Friendship, Texas, where once,
On the iron bridge of Willis Creek, bullboys
Throttled up their trucks to celebrate
The one sad fuck worse off that night than them:
The beaten, black head lolled like a lantern.

At first just looking on, God cocked his head
Toward the faint chatter of satellites beyond,
Then, listening, stepped into the black body of man:
And the light from that body turned them, finally, all to ash:
Such were the miracles of America in those days.

These days, after the dam, the bridge is ruined,
And the cottonmouths hanging from limbs
Over the creek's steep chasm have wandered on.
We watch the sun slip down, and when the butcher bird
Shrieks, a silence follows, a tightening in the dusk.

In the lone mesquite within the canebrake
The litter of bird's prey dangles on its thorns:
Before us the paling sky slumps onto the still, unrivered water.

Mr. Sweatner's Parade

David Daniel

Mr. Sweatner puts his cart before
His snow-eyed mule and pulls them
Down the field roads of Friendship, Texas,
Dragging cans . . .
Wake up! he cries. *Let's get on with it!*
These were the words
My grandfather used to rouse
Him and the other Mexicans who'd lived
In the wetback shed across the cattleguard.
Long ago, Mr. Sweatner's son fell from a tractor
And was baled with the maize,
And a year later his wife and child
Died in childbirth. On that night
He hammered his sixty-five chinchillas
To death and left their skinned bodies
In a pile alive with green flies.
So if he's now come back to gather
The dead Mexicans, and only them,
We ought to forgive his insolence—
Because there is no guilt here—and rather
Follow to where he takes the dead ones:
Some place still not owned, but forever theirs.

The Nineteenth-Century Novel

Eve Grubin

Sometimes I just want to give in and become
the heroine in a great nineteenth-century novel.
An earnest and suffering young woman
who makes the decision that will ruin
the rest of her life.

At the pivotal moment I want
to choose the thing I most desire,
the same thing that will hurt me most.

And then, once the decision has been made,
unlatch the shutter, throw open
the window, cry out into the rain.

Here I am. Living in my own
rent-stabilized apartment, I have feminism,
a job, a therapist, even a few rabbis.
And friends who won't let me plunge
into an epic disaster.

Please, if I could at least be
Elizabeth Bennett in *Pride and Prejudice* who lives
on the precipice of a great disappointment,
on the edge of loneliness and family shame.
To dip just under the surface of the worst
that could happen and then to pull out
just in time.

The Nineteenth-Century Novel II

Eve Grubin

What is it about suffering I still find
compelling?

This indulgence in despair? A glee
in doing the wrong thing, like Eve,
as she reached
for the soft fruit.

A Hunger So Honed

Tracy K. Smith

Driving home late through town
He woke me for a deer in the road,
The light smudge of it fragile in the distance,

Free in a way that made me ashamed for our flesh—
His hand on my hand, even the weight
Of our voices not speaking.

I watched a long time
And a long time after we were too far to see,
Told myself I still saw it nosing the shrubs,

All phantom and shadow, so silent
It must have seemed I hadn't wakened,
But passed into a deeper, more cogent state of dream—

The mind a dark city, a disappearing,
A handkerchief
Swallowed by a fist.

I thought of the animal's mouth
And the hunger entrusted it. A hunger
So honed the green leaves merely maintain it.

We want so much,
When perhaps we live best
In the spaces between loves,

That unconscious roving,
The heart its own rough animal.
Unfettered.

    The second time,
There were two that faced us a moment
The way deer will in their Greek perfection,

As though we were just some offering
The night had delivered.
They disappeared between two houses,

And we drove on, our own limbs
Sloppy after that, our need for one another
Greedy, weak.

.

Self Portrait as the Letter Y

Tracy K. Smith

1.

I waved a gun last night
In a city like some ancient Los Angeles.
It was dusk. There were two girls
I wanted to make apologize,
But the gun was uselessly heavy.
They looked sideways at each other
And tried to flatter me. I was angry.
I wanted to cry. I wanted to bury the pistol,
But I would've had to walk miles.
I would've had to learn to run.

2.

I have finally become that girl
In the photo you keep among your things,
Steadying myself at the prow of a small boat.
It is always summer here, and I am
Always staring into the lens of your camera,
Which has not yet been stolen. Always
With this same expression. Meaning
I see your eye behind the camera's eye.
Meaning that in the time it takes
For the tiny guillotine
To open and fall shut, I will have decided
I am just about ready to love you.

3.

Sun cuts sharp angles
Across the airshaft adjacent.

They kiss. They kiss again.
Faint clouds pass, disband.

Someone left a mirror
At the foot of the fire escape.

They look down. They kiss.

She will never be free
Because she is afraid. He

Will never be free
Because he has always

Been free.

4.
Was kind of a rebel then.
Took two cars. Took
Bad advice. Watched people's
Asses. Sniffed their heads.

Just left, so it looked
Like those half sad cookouts,
Meats never meant to be
Flayed, meant nothing.

Made promises. Kept going.
Prayed for signs. Stooped
For coins. Needed them.
Had two definitions of family.

Had two families. Snooped.
Forgot easily. Well, didn't
Forget, but knew when it was safe
To remember. Woke some nights

Against a wet pillow, other nights
With the lights on, whispering

The truest things
Into the receiver.

5.
A small dog scuttles past, like a wig
Drawn by an invisible cord. It is spring.
The pirates out selling fakes are finally
Able to draw a crowd. College girls,
Inspired by the possibility of sex,
Show bare skin in good faith. They crouch
Over heaps of bright purses, smiling,
Willing to pay. Their arms
Swing forward as they walk away, balancing
That new weight on naked shoulders.
The pirates smile, too, watching
Pair after pair of thighs carved in shadow
As girl after girl glides into the sun.

6.
You are pure appetite. I am pure
Appetite. You are a phantom
In that far-off city where daylight
Climbs cathedral walls, stone by stolen stone.
I am invisible here, like I like it.
The language you taught me rolls
From your mouth into mine
The way kids will pass smoke
Between them. You feed it to me
Until my heart grows fat. I feed you
Tiny black eggs. I feed you
My very own soft truth. We believe.
We stay up talking all kinds of shit.

The Lais of Lost Long Days

Olena Kalytiak Davis

Today I used my new little hummingbird of a poem to get a big old hummingbird of
A bug out the only open, able, window. All my poems are humming-birds, are windows,
Are poems, mostly painted shut. Mostly, suffocate and smile. But, hey, I know a good
Simile when I trap it, under glass. *Like a cup. Discarded. Sordid. YOU COULD*
NOT. The visitors come from all over to see how I can attend to so little for so long. So
Long so sweet! I said that in one of my latest poems. (One of my last.) I have finally got-
Ten permission to repeat myself! Myself, never was one to relive the past, but now
I've seen that one clip many many times. *Because your Face would put out*
Jesus'. Still enjoy it. *That new Grace.* Still think I'm sitting too far back. *Pale. Home-*
Sick. Eye. Still realize it isn't great art. Nothing is. Wire sculpture that. I know, I know,
It's been done. As I am sure someone has already lived this life, this wife, for me. Poor
Fuck. Sick Fish. Lately, I want, (o!), I wish, all my poems to end in, to end with,
Spring. The word, I mean. AND I, COULD I? Lately, I head steadily for, Tread slowly toward, Abelard. Froward, I mean. I mean, Aberdeen.

Stripped from the Waist Up, Love

Olena Kalytiak Davis

and from the waist
down. low.

flankerbacked, love,
flatwise. slow.

flavesent,
and fleecy,
and fletched.

my flews, love.

i am not fleyed, love.
i flicker, love, but i do not
flinch.

flinders of my love, love
flintlocked, flocked.

the floorage, love,
the floss.

flouting.
fluctuant.

here's my flue, love,
here's my fluff.

all the flummery, love.

i am flummox,
i am fluored,

love, i am flush.
flyaway, love,
fly-by-night
with your jibs and squirrels (and yes, your foxes and your fish)

the flyspeck-tacle of it! love,
the traps.

focalized, love,
thru the fogdog and the bank.

a mere foible, love,
and a moist foison, too.

folded, love,
yet quite foliate.

follow me, love,
for i am fond of you, love,

you are parsley and paradise.

i fool.
i foot.

it's in my mouth, love.

i have sent my footboy for you, love,

lambert, lambent. burnt.
o footle!

at a footpace,
at a footpace, love

all stalk and stall.

for you, love,
i forage, love, forasmush love
as is forbade was forbore.
spy my forebearance, love,
eye my force, through ford and fore.

fore and aft love fore and aft.
cast brain bode.

it was foreordained, love
peak and paw.

shadow and shock, love
sight and skin.

mast and sail.

FOR there is LOVE, love,
and there is LOVED.

and there is More.

you are forgiven, love,
i will forgo, love, i will
go, love,
go.

Cellist

Peter Jay Shippy

It's 3:59. My palace is dark.
An unknown knife scratches night's negative

and so the stars appear. *Sorry you're
far away*, says one. I open the fridge

and pop two eyes from their plastic tray.
Freon erases cobwebs from my face.

Earlier in the wine the ballroom Bached
to the suavity of a shoestring octet.

Their bad-mouth organ added that requisite
splenetic cool, that quark that disarms mere

musical felicity. My guests have taken
their quicksands home. *Far away?* It's 4:01.

From the hallway I hear untrammeling
and tiptoe out to lowercase the joint.

My pockets are wet. I'm doggo blind.
I apply dilating drops. I see The Cellist,

a manipulator of cells, waving
to me, waving me *far away*. From what?

It's 3:58. My palace is dark.
An unknown knife scratches night's negative....

Dogs Resembling Their Owner

Peter Jay Shippy

The evening after the world ends
go to Ahab's for a beer or six.

The jukebox hums the old hymns,
the classics: Autechre, Photek

Joe Aristophanes. No one plugs
new tunes or strews their mask.

Sit among the ones so much like you
it's like you alone. You say shit

nothings so no one pays you
no mind, considers you strange

lonely, satisfied. Some pink cheek
check flush buys a round, low-shelf.

The yellow light glows. *Et tu to you*
the house toasts, *This is our story*

and we're stuck to it. Soon
the amending, soon soon comes

the prayers. Then the pruning shears
and pickle jar are sliding to you —

too late for the wiseass — just
clip a digit (plunk) and pass
                          the drowning on.

Three Months, No Kidding

Alison Stine

Because I loved a man who liked skin bare,
even there, and because he is three lovers past now
and I am falling in love with him all over again,

this time in a drunker incarnation. Because he says
he is better than a mirror, which must mean
he will never love me as much as himself,

and because the new razors have three blades,
almost like gills — I have seen them and the song
is three times as sweet. And because I once

broke a glass and let it stay there fractured for days
the way artist friends hung up a smashed clock.
It is not about time, they said. The anniversary

of my stopping used to be so much longer.
Because a girl who was beaten used to do it
but I was never beaten, well, not much, and she says

it is no different from suicide, only you kill yourself
more than once. And because he seems so sad
I want to hurt him, because a lover once hid

everything sharp and if I found it I deserved it,
because I am bare as pigs, because Lucy plucked out
her eyes after tormenting a man and because of this,

is Saint to writers, lamplighters, peddlers, the blind —
in my dreams my body is not the knife, but the eyes.

Salt

Alison Stine

> A woman of twenty-six, while in prison awaiting trial, succeed[ed] in com-
> mitting suicide by introducing about thirty pins and needles in the chest
> region, over the heart. Her method was to gently introduce them, and then
> to press them deeper with a prayer book.
> —*Abnormalities and Curiosities of Medicine*

You were the lover for which I bled. Comfort me
with salt: tears, their silken twin. Understand
I have made my arms doors for you. Listen:
in the quiet cell

she was left with only women's tools—the fat
pin-cushion, muslin, thirty silver jabs to sew
dull squares. She begged for the Bible, knowing
the temper of the hand.

Even the openings which I gave myself
betrayed. They scabbed overnight, star clots. She drove
the points deep with the word, veined leather as black
as her secret down.

All the while I tasted you. But how could I
contain you? There was no slick color until
the third or fourth jag had made its tunnel in.
By then it was sure;

her sampler would be skin. I learned two cuts make
a cross, five is a marker, then the whole of
flesh opens up to be forested—her breast
before mapped with seams,

blood latitude down. I gave everything
of my body. I thought it was punishment
she wanted to escape, guilty, the rope waiting.
It was punishment

she wanted. But I have your salt to comfort me.
Now the stars breaking through the body bared.
Now the blood, tender like touch, flint to the tongue,
and to the mouth, sweet.

NONFICTION

POST ROAD

Sea Monsters

Kate Crane

Tsunamis unfurl slowly from great depths. They are creatures of the open sea, born in places composed of nothing but salt water and sky. Earthquakes and volcanic eruptions give birth to them. Or the collapse of an oceanic island. Events that convince me of Earth's anger. It gnashes its teeth. It wrings the flesh from its hands. It snarls, a bitter old drunk. And with this, a monstrous chain of waves awakes and begins to lurch and leer its way to shore.

The time of the worst wave's arrival is anyone's guess. Waves such as these are uninvited guests that sweep in scathingly, announcing themselves in random succession. Hours can crawl by in between them. It's possible to return too soon, thinking the waves have retreated. Willing them gone, willing calm and one's own warm bed. And then the sea monster rears its most wretched head. Terrible bloomings.

The hapless can be lured in another fashion. Sometimes before a tsunami rushes forth, the sea will inhale, deeply and slowly. The water draws back in a silent siren song, inch by inch until, lo, sand and shells that have endured endless nights and days under cover of water know the sudden choke of sun and sky.

I could be one of the hapless. I could be lured. Newborn beach would stretch out before me, and I would go there; I would answer its call. I would wander onto the wet sand barefoot and turn over shells one by one, fingering their bony twists and ridges. I'd gaze in wonderment at the seabed, with its covers so starkly pulled back. I'd stroll in farther and farther, transfixed. In reverie, in a fog of thought. And at some point I might see the fish at my feet, groaning for the water, shuddering for breath. Shivering, finally, to a halt. Perhaps then I'd grow uneasy.

By then it would be too late. The sea would start to exhale.

I once asked my dad what to do if a tsunami came. Accustomed to such questions from his six-year-old, he looked at me gravely and said, "Well, Prideandjoy, I'd try to ride that wave. Either that or I'd get the hell out of the way."

That was the year I learned to swim.

I've never been graceful on my feet. I'm keenly aware that my body is only too happy to abandon convention and collapse at first chance. One skipped meal and I'm risking a close encounter with concrete. But learning to swim means learning to coordinate one's basic movements and actions in an even more complex way than walking. Stroke and kick and breath. Not simple. The way you cup your hand or point your feet, or the point at which your hand sinks into the water—these things have repercussions. And every so often as I make myself horizontal and push out from the wall, I marvel that I don't sink. I'm struck that my arms and legs and lungs cooperate in such a way that not only am I afloat, but moving forward, with certainty and reasonable speed. My body, so stubborn on land, in water acquiesces.

As a child, I swam often. At 7 a.m. on summer mornings, my mother took me to my swimming lessons, driving me the three blocks to the pool that she and my father had waited a decade to become members to. The big old car would rumble onto the gravel lot. Me in the back seat full of anticipation. My love for the water was searing and bright—nothing could touch it. At that hour, my neighborhood was quiet, and the light was mild. My mind retrieves images steeped in blue and gold and green. Sky, pool, sun, and grass. The snack bar was closed. Diving boards deserted. I think my mother read paperbacks in a beach chair at the side, one careful eye ever upon me, but for some reason I can't picture her there. The image of the pool in my head has swollen and forced out all others.

The pool was always perfectly still then. I don't believe I was ever the first one in, the one who got to break the surface of that great soft mirror. I imagine what it would have been like: my body enters the water like a child-sized rocket, and though my motions are smooth, though I am determined to be one with the water, an army of ripples escapes from my side. The ripples march across the surface, heralding my entrance, rousing this place from the previous night's stasis. From my body comes the day; with a simple sliding motion I bring it on.

We started off in the shallow end. I spent what seemed like weeks at the wall, clutching the pool's cement lip. So clear in my mind are pictures of me and a handful of other children leaning our faces into the water, faces screwed up in terror, blowing those first precious bubbles. We were taught not to clutch breath in puffed cheeks, but to guard it inside our lungs and release it in smart, careful Os. Our teacher stood behind us, waist-deep, while we were submerged to our shoulders. With her there, I knew I was safe. That it was okay to have my back to the water.

As time went on and my lessons progressed, we learned the basic strokes: crawl, breast, side, and back. I was a stellar pupil. In the water, my arms and legs behaved with grace. While the complexity of coordination on dry land was rocket science to me, here I not only kept up, but was a model. The other children flailed about, breath tangling with stroke, frantic arms and legs kicking the water into turbid froth. A telescope pointed into the past might reveal I was only slightly less frantic, my legs kicking up their own fury. But with my mind as the lens, what emerges is quite different. I slide through the pool with nary a splash, not child but water sprite. The world is gone and I swim undetected, undisturbed.

Around the same time as my first swimming lessons, my mother and sister and I began yearly trips to the ocean. Sometimes my father joined us, but not always. I think he had misgivings about the ocean. Though each of us was fair-skinned and all of us burned, his sunburns were the reddest and the meanest. One vacation nearly landed him in the hospital after a nap on the beach gone awry. At first, the umbrella had protected him. But as he slept, the sun moved and stole away the shade. He was left vulnerable. For several nights, my mother tended to him, and the scents of vinegar and Solarcaine infused the air. Maybe it was after that trip that my father didn't come along so often. But when he did, he and I ventured out into the sea together.

I must have been six or seven the first time. He and I set forth from the umbrella bearing a rented rubber raft. Down the sand we strode. He was a very large man, heavy and tall, and my little hand vanished in his grip. The sand changed as we moved toward the water: first the hot, dry kind that clings to sweaty feet, each granule sharp and distinct, confident and golden. Then sand the color of strong dark honey, clumpy and sodden and warm. With each step a footprint was born, deep and distinct until a wave came to fill it, greedily reclaiming our impressions.

The smallest waves greeted us. Timid ambassadors, frothy and white, all foam and sputter. They fawned at our toes and ankles. The first real gushes of water were brisk and no-nonsense, storming our feet and then charging off again, late late late. We were eased into the idea of ocean, gripped by water that quickly receded and left us gazing again at our sandy feet. But now our feet were gone and the water stayed, climbing the trellis of our calves, aspiring to our knees. My father took me to the place where the breakers formed. I was transfixed; the sea moved all around me, churning, its countless facets hurling light like copper pennies. Terror welled up from my stomach and turned my skin to gooseflesh. My teeth chattered as the sea drew breaths and defied gravity to form waves the color of bullets. But my father taught me to move with the ocean. To take its cue. As a wave rolled toward me, he taught me to jump. With his guidance, I learned to intuit the right moment. When it came, I leapt upwards and joined the wave's shore-bound bustle. I soared. The feathery whitecaps snapped into my shoulder blades—salt-water wings.

We stayed for a long time in that place. I'd squeal as the waves rolled us upwards and set us gently back down again. The water was now up to my father's chest. He stood, and I drifted. I was connected to him only by the raft's slim yellow cord, which lay secure in his great strong fist. The possibility that I could be swept away never entered my mind. My father was planted into the seabed. On his neck and shoulders, bits of seaweed gathered, as if the ocean had begun to accept him as one of its own. I held on lightly to the raft, and he held fast to me. I don't recall what we talked about, or if we spoke at all. I no longer have much of a sense of what fathers and daughters say. I just remember the rising and falling of the ocean all around us. I knew then that I loved the sea. It was a fantastical, ominous machine. I imagined that it was powered by a secret, sub-oceanic engine. What else could explain the constant movement, the constant change? Its quiet swells and vociferous tumblings, or its whispers and roars? Eventually my dad would let me go, and I would cling to my raft, waiting for a wave. It propelled me to shore, and I was bathed in glee. This was flight. Sand and shell bloodied my legs as I came to rest. Giddy, I'd beg to do it again.

That summer I learned to swim, and I made my first acquaintance with the ocean, the great beast that a swimming pool so sadly mimics. I took it all in stride. Small children can adapt. They're not so cemented in their ways, so sure as adults of the way the world is or should be.

(There were no more trips to the beach once my father had been murdered.)

A year and a half ago, I had not swam regularly in years. This was by no conscious choice; life had led me away. As I hurtled into my teens, I stopped going to the pool. All of us did. Sometimes my mother made half-hearted visits, but ventured there only at dusk. She'd sit at the side. As the light died, she'd let her feet absorb the chill of the chlorinated water. Eventually she gave up the membership.

Nighttime brought me back. Over the course of a few months, my dreams filled with water. Once I found my dream-self submerged in the midst of a shipwreck, surrounded by bodies drifting downwards like leaden autumn leaves. Shards of broken vessel shimmered like tinsel. I was aware of fires raging on the surface, and yearned to shoot upwards and lick the air alongside the flames. But I'd forgotten how to swim. I shot from sleep gasping, lungs pounding, chest heaving. Trying to capture breath. This waking was a terrible journey. My limbs were lost to me—arms and legs no longer mine made turbulent snarls of the bed linens, ceasing only when I was fully ensnared. I was held fast by the bed sheets, not certain if I could breathe, certain that the sound of cars on the street below was actually the din of approaching swells. I waited on obliteration. But the only water in that small bedroom was my sweat. There was no drowning, only shaking.

Another night I paced the edge of the pool in which I'd learned to swim. Here was that place, the familiar L-shape, the numbered demarcations of depth hovering just below the water's surface. I found my reflection in that watery expanse. We stared at one another, wordless. Gradually I noticed a shark, formidable in size, coasting under the water, slicing through my reflection now and again, grey razor. It moved through the water but made no sound, created no ripples. I knew I could not join it. I knew that to share the water with such a swimmer could be fatal. Yet closer and closer to the edge moved my feet. That shark tainted the water, lent it a hostile scent, but nonetheless I yearned to fall in quietly, thought perhaps I could go for a time undetected.

I don't know what becomes of me in this dream. It continues, but I wrench myself out. I leave my dream-self deciding whether or not to swim with a shark, wondering why I dream these dreams. On nights like these I would cling to my then-partner, she who slumbered ever onwards, encased in a vessel of sleep far sturdier than my own. During those nights I sought solidity—pillow, partner, cold hard wall. I never found it. My bedroom was a place of treachery, and nights crashed around my head, relentless.

Sharks and shipwrecks in the night tend to follow one into day. And off of one another they feed, until what is dreamt and lived become indistinguishable. This sometimes means sitting in an office in a skyscraper knowing that a wall of waves is on the verge of splintering through the door. Sometimes this means falling asleep at your desk and encountering friends and coworkers, but sour, sullied versions. These wraiths rifle through one's packed-away worries and fears as if through a trunk of old clothes. They hold them up and, jeering, make a mocking display. So at night what is trusted falls upon one; what is good in daylight is reborn dark and brutal. This is a form of sleep deprivation. Right sleep is a deep velvet falling, a warm, safe burrowing. This safe place had been vandalized, exposing me to an almost nightly pummeling.

Somewhere around this time I drifted back to the water. I was reaching into myself. I remembered this thing that I had loved as a child, this thing I'd been good at. I didn't know if I could still swim, but I felt I had to try. The ground at my feet seemed less stable every day. I was still feeling the aftershocks of a two-year-long string of upsets: a wrongful termination and subsequent lawsuit; a major surgery that required over a month of recovery; a broken foot and a month of crutches in a cruel New York August. Even as I began to dismantle a four-year relationship, and consequently my home, I was still picking my way through old rubble. My breathing had grown increasingly shallow, and I think there were times when I would just altogether forget to breathe. My heart would pound in protest, and I would fill my lungs only in afterthought. Perhaps it wasn't so conscious then, but I knew that swimming would necessitate breathing. That I would have to focus on the air that entered and departed my lungs. That otherwise I might drown.

So last winter I swam heavily. I was hungry and full of longing, desperate to get somewhere faster than I could possibly go. I was a thousand pumping wings, breathless with their beating. Deaf with their thunder. So badly I wanted to fly, to press a fast-forward button and flash ahead a year or two or five. I was overflowing with a nervous energy akin to rocket fuel, and infuriated at the necessary slowness of forward motion. My skin fairly rippled with energy. I wanted to go, go, go. And that electricity crackled through my veins for months. I walked my neighborhood feverishly at night, sometimes for hours at a time. I reveled in the night sky, in the buildings and streets and passersby. In this way, I exhausted myself. I walked so that I could sleep at night. And I swam so I could get through the days. At one point I took an entire week off of work and swam every day. A voice in my head had told me in no uncertain terms to stop everything and swim. I listened.

When I first enter the water, I linger at the wall. I've never been able to step in and push off immediately. Descending the ladder is leaving one state for another, and I find this unsettling no matter how often I swim. My body takes stock of the water's temperature, the smell of the chlorine, the sounds of other swimmers propelling themselves through the lanes. I adjust my goggles. Invariably, my legs conduct a series of languid kicks and shakes, while my arms lock into quiet akimbo. These movements are a ritual of inquiry, a pattern both of curiosity and reluctance. Slipping into the water is an uneasy homecoming. The sensations are familiar: the chill of the water as it soaks my suit and skin, the rock and smack of ersatz waves, the bottom of the pool against the bottom of my feet. Soothing and seductive. I like it here. But while I enter the pool conscious that I am just a visitor, a sense of urgency wells up from my bones. Compulsions, like stage whispers, sift into my thoughts. Something in the wings says stay. Slide beneath the surface and remain.

My lungs are left out of this. Breath is an understudy on closing night that, forgotten, fades from the picture.

The first lap holds singular bliss. There is nothing like those few minutes, immersed, embraced. A certain softness reigns. Some nights when I am especially tired or the day has been inordinately hard and I have been away from my bed a particularly long time, I slip into bed and find my hands and feet tracing patterns beneath the flannel sheets. They act alone, autonomous, brushing to and fro in mute revel. As if there were no finer fabric than that worn flannel. My hands drift and dance like rice-paper pendulums. They make small angels. It's like this when I swim. My two-legged awkwardness falls away. Like a sea turtle—what on land lumbers in water soars. Like that.

Several years ago, I swam naked at a friend's house in south Jersey. There were a lot of people there, many that I didn't know. But it had rained hard that night, and a thick fog hung over and around the pool and house and surrounding trees. The moon was nearly full; it illuminated the fog, and I was bathed in the subsequent hollow blueness. That night is etched in my mind. Black branches scraped against a washed-out sky. Voices were reduced to a murmur behind me. I could have been completely alone. As it was, I was the only one who cared to stay in the water for any length of time. My other friends stole in and out in a nervous pack, eager to dress, giggling to cover up their discomfort. My own boldness astonished me. I wasn't at that point in my life very comfortable with my body; moreover, I was painfully shy. But beneath the water, my breasts and hips and legs were white armor. From my neck down, I was transformed. Changed into something that belonged as much to the water as it did to me. It was early summer, and the water was icy and sharp. My lungs groaned and grew cool within my chest; it was hard to breathe. Even as my legs kicked and spun, I worried that the cold would seep under my skin—I would slow and then cease to move and sink, and somehow I wasn't sure anyone would notice. Yet water lends a weightlessness that's uncanny in contrast to its own downward pull. Your body says, fly, fly!, but the water would drown given a chance. No malice— nothing but the pull.

That night I was a water sprite all over again. I suppose I strive for this to some degree each time I swim. At my pool in Brooklyn, the end of every swim approaches trauma. It is jarring to leave the pool, to go from swimmer-in-water to walker-on-land. My body had adapted. The water was warm on my skin. It pressed against me, seeped inside me, filled every orifice and anointed every contour. My knees were strong and solid, my legs were sure. I kicked with precision. I belonged.

Ascending the ladder changes everything. The water recoils from my skin in disdain. I'm left shivering, skin shriveled, legs rubbery, bewildered at the way the room spins around me. To be upright is alarming. How can I stand over five feet tall and not tumble over? So much noise— splashes, the blare of a shitty radio, small talk at the wall. All echoing like a high school gym. Seeds of panic crack open in my chest.

It seems that I became too comfortable in that other realm. And now this one metes out its punishment. Rightfully so? I overstepped my bounds, tried to pass for native in a place where I can only ever be a guest. Standing at the top of the ladder, I'm in between two worlds. And I can't have both. Without gills, there's only one way to stay in the water.

During the day the pool is often deserted, and light drifts down lazily through the massive skylight. Here is this little patch of water in a concrete box in the middle of Brooklyn. The sun shines down onto it, indifferent. But even on a grey day, watery light descends onto that pool and brings the sky a little closer to the swimmers. A dim parallel to ocean swimming, or even lake swimming, where you're a thin layer of being between a body of water and the sky.

On the fourth of July, I went to Coney Island with friends. The beach and boardwalk were teeming with life. It was chilly and bleak, but a few of us went swimming anyway. The debris was formidable. T-shirts and bottles, scraps of paper and bits of sandwiches made a soggy lace at the water's edge. The ocean licked these little bits of lives in assessment— claim or reject? We waded through all of it, lamenting the filth and the cold. I didn't mind it so much. The ocean on my eyes crowded all other things from my mind. I hadn't seen the Atlantic in well over a year. While my friends talked around me, I gave myself over to the sea that stretched out before me. Heaven, heaven.

This time last year, I dreamt that I saw my father's body pulled from Curtis Bay, a foul, fetid patch of water in South Baltimore. He was face down, but I could see his hair, and he was wearing one of my work shirts, winter-weight linen, coarse and brown like burlap. I woke from this dream alone in my bed, pinned down by the pounding of grief and loss. I was stricken with sadness to leave him alone in that brackish pool. I couldn't pull him to shore. He was dead, and there was nothing for me to do. I could only move forward. This time last year I was waiting for September. For the fourteenth anniversary of his death, the one that meant I'd been alive longer without a father than with. Now the fifteenth looms. (It was unexpected. I went to bed a child and woke up to death.)

I watched a friend dive headlong into a wave. For a moment she was flawless, a fluid tuck of black hair and sun-browned shoulders. She arched into a breaker. Disappeared. My heart pounded out each moment she was gone, and I realized I'd stopped breathing. So much can happen. So much can happen in the span of two moments. A familiar numbness began to climb my calves, reaching for my stomach and lungs. It was cold, and the sky was getting darker.

But then she plunged forth, salt water streaming from her face and shoulders and chest. She was laughing, decrying the cold through bluing lips and chattering teeth. Though the water still held her from the waist down, she'd returned from the waves, bearing laughter and breath. I relaxed and felt the numbness retreat.

I waded out towards her, passed her, trudged along until I could barely touch bottom. I rose and fell with the sea. Though it was chilly, I was sweating, and I realized that my sweat and the sea water were indistinguishable. I looked down and found that my body was gone. From the shoulders down, I belonged to the murky waters of the Atlantic.

I accepted this. And I accept uncertainty, at least for now. I know that I share the water with a shark at any given moment. But staying on the beach is not an option. I can't stand the feel of hot sand on my feet. I can't stand to sit at the side and watch the waves rise and fall. I'm drawn to this place; I'm drawn to this water. I give myself over. The ocean is my mother. I stretch out and wait. ✧

The Middle-Aged Man and the Sea

Larry O'Connor

We are on a winding road along the Pacific Coast of Mexico for what seems like forever. M. and I are never more than a few miles from the sea, but it's spare country; our views are confined to roadside pines and the occasional tourist tree, a fat, red, foreign-looking variety with bark that peels. Rest, M. says, it's going to be a big day. I catch a glimpse of the water around a bend. The sea is not the roiling, windswept black water of the north. Or the smooth turquoise of a tropical lagoon. It is lapis blue, with white caps, the color of lakes at home, and I shudder with terror.

M. convinced me it would be all right when I reluctantly agreed to go on this trip. We are to meet teachers at the local marine institute and join them on their morning run to ancient fishing grounds. For centuries these people have lived and worked in the same way. Gringos, M. tells me, have never seen such a thing.

The fishermen at the water's edge don't look like any teachers I have ever seen. Men with hands like those in a Siquerios mural lift crates and tools into a boat, a long flat affair with no cabin and an outboard motor. Their feet, too, are huge and quick. They dash about barefoot, pivoting, twisting, making soft little leaps. The beach is filthy, and there are no palapas for sunbathers, only rows of empty crosspieces used for drying the day's catch. A battered colorless lifejacket is left on the sand for me. My feet are sinking into the wet sand.

Across the blur of brown humanity, I see M.; she is already on board the small boat, which is moving up and down in the waves. So beautiful in her white shorts and nautical top. Yet she may as well be a million miles away. Put it on, she motions. No one else is wearing a lifejacket, I stammer. A man pushes the lifejacket into my chest and scrambles ahead of me. I put it on.

Water doesn't exactly revolt me. I shower every day. I like the rain. Even my garden plants sense me coming. But miles and miles, wave upon wave, of deep water is another thing. I get weak in the knees just looking at the open sea. I throw up. I'm a hydrophobe.

Reformed drunks know what I'm talking about. They treat their fear through confession—I am John, and I am an alcoholic. My father had a different idea. "Face your fears, boy," he said. "Sink or swim." Those who have survived near-misses with death say at the moment of decision—

the firing mechanism of a pistol misfires, a bolt of lightning hits—they remember every detail: the smell of the air, the quality of the light on a leaf. Arm hairs and skin pores turn into millions of tiny receptors. Fear is the cattle prod of memory. Before an encounter with water over my head I am crackling of feelings. Fear is a cattle prod of memory. It can be a great mobilizer. Or it can make you crazy.

The boat is rocking in the waves. A big hand pushes my back and another jerks my arm and I'm in the stern. The water is not blue but black, like coal. We are leaving shore. Dazed and breathless, I stand until a powerful little man pulls me down to avoid being pummeled by a wave. Soaked to the skin and gripping the seat beneath me, I am the toxic cargo, a gringo in an obsolete lifejacket, scared to death in three and a half feet of water.

I feel laughing eyes on me, but as the spray lifts I look up instead to the gray eyes of an old man. The old man is dressed in rags, sitting cross-legged on the floor of the boat, gazing at me. We hit another wave and water drenches us all. I tuck myself into a ball to protect against the next one.

I am nine years old and hugging my knees, sitting on a wide flat stone before a river. For the previous three weeks that summer, we ten boys in the swim class had made good progress. We could open our eyes underwater, bob, do the dead man's float. Today would be the big test. Before us lay a patch of deep water, a foot or two over our heads. One by one the boys swam across, slapping the water like disabled seahorses. They had all passed me by, jumped ahead, did their first swim, and squealed as they reached the other side.

I had never liked the lessons. I was doing it for Mother. She didn't swim. A Depression baby from a large working-class family, Mother married young and was a martyr for her children. What she didn't have we would have. My instincts clashed with hers. When a family photographer took the first picture of my sister, brother, and me, I stubbornly resisted looking in the direction I was told. People make up their own minds, I believed. But everyone should learn to swim, I told myself. What was wrong with me?

I grew up with a dream that I was being sucked down into ooze. Not deep water but bottomless mud. The most obvious Freudian interpretation is that the mud symbolized a sexual coming of age. Sex equals change equals death. But such views were worlds away from me when I was a boy. Night after night I woke up in a cold sweat, shivering in fright.

The patch of water was no longer than the size of an average man, but it didn't matter; I wouldn't budge. One counselor looked at me in disgust, another gave me a little push. "C'mon! C'mon!" the boys jeered from the other side of the sliver of deep water. I couldn't move. Finally, I gathered my towel, and without saying a word or shedding a tear, got on my bike and rode away.

Looking up is out of the question. I've found that if I sit hunched forward, my head in my lap, that I can stop the gorge of vomit from rising in my throat, keep the trembling to a minimum.

The man who rescued me from the wave is sitting on the lap of the boatman, and at turns they whisper like lovers, then laugh and laugh. The old man has gone to sleep, resting against the stocky leg of a big-headed man, the captain, it seems.

It is not the open sea, a thin man who turns out to be a scientist explains, but a bay, so the waves are rarely high. He places a small eyepiece in my hand, a temperature gauge that is used to find the most likely channel for the choicest fish to swim in. Now we're traveling to that place. Relax, he says, patting the gray humpback of my lifejacket, how do you say it? Take it easy.

I was on the road when I met M., the woman who would be my wife. In my single days, my travels took me to mountain trails, to the blazing sun of the Mojave, to Alaskan glaciers. M. and I met at a conference where the only water was in the fountain of our hotel lobby. It wasn't until after we were married that she came to know the extent of my fear. I quoted Spalding Gray to her, that I preferred hysterical misery to a common unhappiness. I joked that I was so afraid of water that as a boy I didn't even have wet dreams. M., an avid swimmer, wasn't laughing.

The painted wood of the gunwale seems to give way under the pressure of my handgrip. The sound of huge scissorsbirds is everywhere. Loud, snapping, and insistent, unyielding in their pathetic aggression, the black mangy sea birds sense a meal, would bite a fisherman's hand for a scrap of catfish.

Two fingers are missing from the old man's hand, I notice, as he pulls his rags even tighter about his bony frame. The wind spray, squawking birds, and limitless depth of the sea sicken me as the old man rests, his body swaying to the rhythm of the boat.

I'd never met my Cousin Bruce, but he was a good swimmer. But that didn't stop him from drowning before I was born. He was on board a freighter, and somehow he lost his balance and fell. His body was never found. I don't know if it was because of Bruce—in my family we never talk of such things—but Mother, her sister and brothers, their children, and their children's children are terrified of deep water, cannot swim a single stroke.

Cousin Bruce was the first of our family to work on the boats. Only the privileged in our town were chosen to work on the Great Lakes, and

Bruce was the best of our breed: a hockey player in the headlines, a handsome and gentle young man. He'd walk into a room and people in town whispered among themselves, looked his way. Everyone loved Bruce. Mother, his adoring aunt, most of all.

I've imagined Bruce's first thought after the fall was that he couldn't feel his feet in his boots. His arms moved rhythmically in wide circles, but his feet weren't cooperating. Numb from the fall and cold, his legs moved like an eagle's wings in an updraft. A perfect sweep but too slow to keep him suspended, and he began to sink. No matter how hard he tried, he couldn't get his legs to kick. Finally, exhausted from the struggle, he yielded, and with the force of the current, his arms and legs spread wide, Cousin Bruce floated like a slowly revolving starfish down the current and through the frigid water into the depths of the lake.

The boat we are approaching smells like a sewer. Five crew members climb aboard in a single movement and fan out along its side. Repulsed by the stink, I get up unsteadily and bump two fishermen with my lifejacket. They nearly lose their balance, go overboard. The boatman's friend points to the water over the side of the boat, makes pulling-like gestures, sticks his thick finger into my chest. "You, you will help us bring up the net." I am flabbergasted, and I shake my head no, you must be kidding. M. is at the front of the boat talking to the scientist, trying not to catch my eye. Surely, there has been some mistake, another man can take my place. But every man is at his station, preparing to bring up the net. Only the old man is lying down, fast asleep.

Twice a day for as long as people can remember the boats have been going out like this. One panga, or open work boat, is moored at the fishing grounds where the net is fixed. Before leaving each time, the fishermen, muttering prayers and crossing themselves, open the enormous trapdoor of the fishing net. It's as if it were St. Peter's Gate. Or foreskin, the boatman's friend says. He is holding his hand before him suggestively. Like pulling back foreskin.

The men in the stinking skiff close the net, hoping that since their last visit a bounty will appear. Gringo, the net needs to come up. Start hauling the net.

My father is a barrel-chested man who, when I was growing up, would stand in the waves of Lake Huron and play catch with me. I'd be in shallow water and throw a rubber ball to my father where the waves broke, thirty, forty feet away. I was nervous in water and my father, who had a loud, mean voice, which got louder and meaner when he felt neglected, only made me more nervous. So weekend after weekend we played a silent game of catch in cold water until we got bored and stopped.

One weekend Father buried me up to my neck in sand. While others were swimming in the lake, I wanted to be in a hole in the earth. I liked the symmetry of it, being immersed if not in a Great Lake, then in its shoreline. My arms were at my side, where the sand had been packed in tight. Cool grains of sand pressed against me from my toes to the hollow of my throat.

My head sprouted like an asparagus—remote and exotic. Before me were bird tracks, windblown husks, dead pine needles. I was the boy with the brains and ambition. In years to come, valedictorian, the first boy in the family to go to college, be a journalist, a writer. Today I would be immersed in earth, land, surrounded in comfort. Never water, never into the dark blue. The land is everything. The land will set me free.

Suddenly, like a light switch thrown, I couldn't breathe. My arms couldn't move, my feet only dug in deeper. When Shelley drowned, the non-swimmer went "arms at his side, submissive through the waves." I sensed my chin digging even deeper into the sand.

I was losing consciousness when Baby Bruce, a little boy who was named after Cousin Bruce, suddenly appeared before me. Eskimos believe the spirit of the best of the dead live on in their namesakes, so they never name their young after another living soul. In this way, the line between the living and dead is never broken. "Bruce," I whispered, "Get someone to help." Bruce stared at me, and then I blacked out.

People too drunk to swim must have listened to Bruce and come to pull me out because the next thing I knew my father was standing above me—not touching me but watching me as I was lying motionless on a scratchy sofa, faking sleep.

On the fishing grounds the panga is remarkably still. Slowly, I rise to my feet and am surprised that I do not feel ill. Up and down the length of the boat, men are pulling up the net. There are no fish, only the biggest, heaviest net I have ever seen in my life. If this is fishing, then groundskeeping is baseball. Help, I could help, but I can't seem to lift my hands. It is as if I am underwater, falling, a dead weight.

Something is tickling my leg. I turn every few seconds, but I can't see anything wrong. It's a scrape at the top of my calf, the fleshy part. Is the boatman's friend playing a trick? No, he is at his station, pulling at the net. Sometimes it's a rough scrape, almost a sting. I swing around quickly, but I notice nothing.

Suddenly I'm pulled backward with a yank. The boatman's friend holds the wet strap of the lifejacket to my face, while his free hand is pulling in the net. The strap was dangling against the back of my leg. Now sit down, he motions abruptly, sit down and get out of the way. We have work to do.

Everybody's got a story. There are things you can't run away from, hide, distort. Summer always comes around. Meet you at the beach. Bring a towel, your fears. Tie a noose around your neck. As a boy I couldn't even say it. I don't swim. I say it now. I don't swim. I've practiced the manner in which it's said, so it comes out like, I don't smoke, I don't take drugs, I don't speak Norwegian. Still, a stain of failure, of weakness, remains.

To fail water is to fail a great test. Annette Kellerman, an English swimmer at the turn of the twentieth century, said mastery of water shows how we meet the unknown. "I assume no adventurer or discoverer ever lived who could not swim," she said. Others said this unknown is not so mysterious. John Cowper Powys said a human being feels drawn backward, down a long series of avatars into the earlier planetary life of animals. To be immersed in water is to feel the succor of mother. Psychologists will tell you swimmers are characterized as having loving, nurturing mothers, distant cold fathers. To be separate, an individual on land, is a man's world. Water, a woman's world.

Once I rowed a boat into a lake and M. swam in deep water. She approached the boat and slipped off her water shoes and handed them to me one by one as if she were suspended in air. Soaked through and curved by the shape of her feet, the shoes lay on the floor of the boat. I was revolted and aroused in equal parts. I wanted to raise the shoes to my lips and drink the water, truly feel M., the swimmer. I imagined our bodies intertwined in water, moving freely. After a moment's pause, though, I shuddered and returned to my task, rowing the boat, regarding solemnly M.'s steady stroke as she headed to shore.

For years, I identified with Richard Kimball, the Fugitive. And Superman, the orphan boy, sent into space by his parents, leaders on a doomed planet, where all life vanished. I preferred the Fugitive, though, a man falsely accused, who was trying to find answers. It seemed to me that Superman was running away from his past by performing mighty tasks of goodwill. He was basically a loner, a loser. He just couldn't face the fact that he was alone, and he was so busy he never realized how lonely he really was.

As a young adult I was more like Superman, aimlessly running away —to islands. I liked the punishing self-loathing irony of it, a non-swimmer living for months on end with nothing but water all around. In Huahine, an outer Tahitian island, I'd lay on a branch overhanging a green cove. For weeks I camped on an isolated shore, drinking cheap vodka, reading Russian novels, contemplating the ocean. Clear shallow water showed the thinnest of ripples, stretching for miles to the shore of a remote spit. But never did I even step into the warm water. Tahitians and travelers alike, those who would come down my way, skirted me as they would a crazy person, whispered and pointed as they passed.

Later, on another island, I stood in a field of string beans, hooking up irrigation pipes for a Tasmanian farmer. In Tasmania, the sea is always on the wind. Salt spray transforms sunsets into Turner landscapes, the air into elixir. Working in that field in the clothes I'd borrowed from John Waterworth, the farmer, I felt something deep inside me fill with light and understanding. It was not about home, or love, or friendship. I felt the presence of the sea all around me, and I was at peace.

Before returning to work for a time, I stopped =on Prince Edward Island to visit my oldest friend. I'd been away a year and collected various treasures—shells from Huahine, a pocket watch from my Tasmanian friend. I'd taken rolls and rolls of film. In a little bolsa I never let out of my sight, I kept my writings and drawings, the journals of my trip, and only these were not stolen from me. Everything that I'd collected in my far-away travels was lifted from a storage room of the island's only luxury hotel. Penniless, with no prospects, and only a sidebag of notes, poems, and drawings, I felt for the first time in my travels what it meant to be free.

Wherever you go, you bring yourself with you. I'm a middle-aged man now, but still I go back to those moments of clarity, the salt air in my breast on a farm in Tasmania. "Face your fears, boy. Sink or swim." Eventually, the Fugitive cleared himself, frustrated his pursuers. My search is hardly over. Mother's love isn't buried at the bottom of the sea where I can't go.

Schools of silver-gray conefish, too small to keep, are stuck in the mesh of the net. I tell myself their big eyes do not register anything. They are flesh and instinct, nothing more. Thousands of lidless eyes are the first living things to emerge from the murk of the ocean. I begin to breathe easily again, feel my hands at my sides. There is no telling how long the conefish have been there, snagged in the mesh.

I move toward the boatman's friend and ask if I can help. Pull the net by putting your fingers inside the mesh and you're asking for trouble, he shows me. Instead, gather the netting in a loose fist first and then pull back the whole ball with both hands. Slip a finger in the net and the weight shifts, you could lose the finger. "Como el," he says, jerking his thumb in the direction of the old man, and I begin to wonder if he is like me, another piece of unwanted cargo, a man not as old as I had thought but too careless to be trusted.

My back aches, a muscle in my upper thigh twinges, but all is quiet as we pull on the net, bringing it up inch by inch from the deep. We work like this for what seems a long time. Suddenly, the net stiffens and drops. It is all we can do to hold on under the weight of hundreds upon hundreds of jumping, thrashing fish. A ton, more than a ton, they say. In such numbers as I had never seen before, fish topple into the boat. Flesh slaps like a million hands on a million wet bodies. Our partner boat moves in closer, and the catch at the bell of the net gathers into a flopping, gleaming silver mountain. The boatman's friend smiles as if he will burst and even though I feel my shoulder lock, the bug-like flick of the lifejacket strap, and a sharp pain in my lower back, I let go the loudest "YAHOO!" I can muster. "YAHOO!" I scream again until I am as red as a lobster and the crew begins to wonder just what they have brought on board.

As a boy the only stories I was told were in Sunday school about fishermen in rags who stooped over their catches, never straying from the task. I'm thinking of these stories as I watch the old man rise and pick through the fish in the hold. He selects the silver ones with the rose spots and puts them in a cloth bolsa and tosses flat sunfish into the sea.

My arms are worn out, as if they are twice as long as normal, and a muscle in my lower back feels tight. I move carefully, while the boatman's friend is running his hand up the hairy leg of the boatman and laughing, pointing at me. Humpback gringo has brought us luck. Humpback gringo, the good luck charm. He pulls me close and rubs his sandpaper face into my cheek, my nose, my eyes. I'm wet with mucus and tobacco juice and seawater.

The Mexicans have stopped their work and are watching as their captain holds a blowfish. Flattened milky spines are stretched into one long supple muscle with a hole, sucking air. It grows enormous, a wide flat paddle of flesh, so thin that light reflects through it. The huge man throws the blowfish, whirling like an ameba, for the scissorsbirds to catch in their snapping beaks and shred into a bloody mess in the wink of an eye.

Next, the captain stands in the middle of the boat, straddling the mounds of squirming fish, and bites into the flesh of a raw one. I don't know if the fish were a particularly rare breed, or a sacrifice more easily made, but the man bites again and again into the living thing until blood spurts over his wet beard and dribbles down his face. Others do the same, up and down the boat, as the blood of the catch sprays into the air. I don't bite the flesh, but I, too, grab a fish and thrust it into my face. We throw the carcasses into the air and a battle rages again among the scavenger birds for the remains.

"Sushi," the leader cries, as clear as day. "Sushi."

*

The boatman's friend and I are both leaning against the boat's wall, our legs elevated to escape the sting from the spine of the stray catfish that flop in the hold beneath us.

Suddenly, a little before we are due to pull into the harbor, the boatman cuts the engine. I hear a splash, and look up to see the old man floating on the surface of the water. Only his red neck and white hair are dry, while beneath him layers of threadbare cloth undulate in the dark water like the costume of a palace dancer.

At first he treads water, moving his arms and legs so much like a fish that for a moment I believe in mermen, in white-bearded men who move through the water like gods. Before he begins his strokes toward shore, he glances in my direction. He is not wide-eyed like a fish, but at peace, contemplative. Then he turns and swims ever so slowly, kicking toward home. The bolsa full of fish that he will sell in his village he holds in one arm while he does the breaststroke with the other.

For a long moment the fishermen watch to be certain that the ancient swimmer is on his way. Then the motor is restarted, and we head toward shore.

Under the weight of the midday catch, the boat rides heavily in the water, a mere foot or so from the walls of the stern. I let my hand dip into the sea. The water feels cool like silk to the touch. ✧

Third Street. Stambaugh, Michigan: Late Spring, 1972

Chad Faries

Third Street was completely tunneled out of elm branches, and we lived at an opening, our apartment half in and half out, depending on the direction of wind and which of the four rooms we felt like settling in. My room was almost always in the shade because of the thick trunk that ran past the window. On some evenings night bears crawled up and scratched at the window with their claws, and I let them in to part my hair.

Mother was not only a mother now; she was a sexual being again. She was loving off and on like a lighthouse spotlight briefly shining on an island of screaming gulls. She'd thought she'd lost the magic of a full hip sway and pouting lips, her heavy blue eyes full of love letters. She soothed her stretch marks with my baby oil. She'd rub us both down every evening, preparing me for bed and herself for lovemaking. Since I couldn't see the sun, I counted the days by the comings and goings of men. Lying in my oil-slicked sheets, I was lulled to sleep by the chiming of the door bell and the beats of boots clomping up the stairs to the living room where a man would be greeted by a scratchy Joni Mitchell album and a high-pitched pucker from Mother's sea-ship lips that often floated down my arms to the tips of my ecstatic, waving fingers. And that is what I imagined as I lay there, knowing it was night because another man had come. I held my arms up in the dark, wondering what my hands were holding, then floated off to sleep.

"I want you," is what woke me up most of the time. I understood that. It drifted in from the next room. I thought she was calling for me, but tonight it was John Lowden. I saw him once in the daytime as I was looking out the window when I was supposed to be napping. Through the branches I saw a beam of sun striking his big red truck and his silver belt buckle. The light from the buckle struck Mother's cheek and illuminated her dimple that was nestled in a drop of shade. I was happy she was smiling. I was happy I was smiling. That simple stretching of the lips seemed to soothe my crooked teeth that just couldn't manage to come out right. She was saying "I want you" then, too, but without words, and I saw a brief semblance of what might be called love. Then a bird flew into the tree and I thought about that, and a red tricycle. I fell asleep with my chin resting on the window sash.

I don't know if John Lowden was a good man, or if any men were good. And I didn't know what she wanted him for. Did she want to feed him or give him a bath? What usually followed "I want you" was confusing sounds of what I came to know as some sort of ecstasy, which, at one-

and-a-half-years-old, I could only equate with jumping up and down in my Johnny Jumper until the elastic was about to snap and I was out of breath.

With John Lowden the sounds came again, but much heavier, like the wind that had pushed open the vertical window a little bit and frazzled my hair. In this ecstasy it sounded like she was hurting. Her breath was so heavy I confused it with the wind. It whirled in under the door and warmed me a little but wasn't enough to pacify my concern that she was really hurting and needed me. She whimpered like the wounded puppy I watched get struck by a car out the same window that was opening wider now, like a huge mouth. Things got really loud and I began to think that all the men had been secretively beating her and she kept taking it, while I just lay there wondering. I started to get really hot and itchy. My ears swelled so big that I could hear Gramma and all my aunts being beaten from across town. I was waiting for the night bear to come and itch me a little, part the hair from my eyes. I thought that if she would just come and cuddle me that the bear would part her hair, too.

One itch for each sound manifested somewhere on my baby-oiled body until I couldn't take it any more and let out the biggest fucking bear roar I could possibly muster up; and I understood what a fucking roar was. So here we all were in the house with four rooms situated in a schizophrenic shade, in a city with four thousand women screaming, and roofs lifting off at the moon like rockets. Everything was clear in the moonlight, and I twisted out of bed, full of itch and oil, and slid into the living room to make some sense of ecstasy.

And there she stood, naked, radiating moonlight. It was the way her shoulders shook and what they were shaking for.

"Go back to bed, honey, everything is alright," she said without a trace of sorrow.

"What the hell does he want," John Lowden boomed.

"Fuck You!"

"Sorry!" he exclaimed.

But I was still roaring, and hot, looking at John Lowden without his belt buckle. I itched my sea-dream arms until they bled salt water and oil slicks.

"Oh my God!" Mother panicked as she stared at my arms.

"What the fuck's a matter with him? Are you alright kid?"

"Fuck you!" I said, falling in love with language.

She rushed over to me and examined my arms.

"Some kind of bites?" John Lowden said.

"I don't fucking know. Put your clothes on," she told him. A gust blew in from my room. "Oh honey, you're so hot."

"But it's freezing in his room—is the window open?"

She picked me up, and we entered my room where the window's big mouth was panting wide open and the wind rustled in the trees where birds pretended to sleep, silently watching. John Lowden trailed behind, stumbling as he tried to put his pants back on, his buckle chinking against his zipper.

"Bugs!" John Lowden said, "That tree's full of them I bet! He got eaten alive!"

I still roared, and would continue to roar until John Lowden fastened that magic buckle and descended the staircase, taking back the footsteps that had lulled me to sleep hours earlier.

"Oh shit," Mother said to herself as she bobbed up and down with me hot in her arms. "Don't worry, honey we'll call Gramma ... I said put your fucking clothes on and get out of here!"

She held me in one arm and picked up the phone with the other. John Lowden left. The plastic phone dial wouldn't turn fast enough. I quieted down a bit when I heard the red truck fire up. I got lost in the sound of the engine idle while Gramma finally answered, rescued from her own screaming.

"Chad's all hot and full of bumps! I don't know what happened—I think the window blew open and there were some bugs in the tree that ate him up or something. I don't know. I don't know what to do. Can you come?"

I don't know what Gramma was saying on the other end. The roofs had come back from the moon and settled in their proper places, and my hearing was normal again as I rested limp in Mother's arms. She brought me into the bathroom. Those spots were all over me now. She put me in the tub and hosed me down with cold water to break my temperature. I was in love again, a good love, like when lemons and matches are in your stomach. I just sat there awhile, not talking because it felt right. The itch subsided under the stream of cool liquid, and I imagined a water slide that led out my window and down into the street. I slid down it. I imagined running back up the stairs, and sliding down again. I imagined it faster and faster until I was just a circular blur of entering and exiting.

"Chad!" I opened my eyes to the women. "Look at him! I told you! What the hell is it?" I didn't pay much attention to anything.

"Well it sure the hell isn't bug bites," Gramma said. "It's chicken pox."

My first disease wasn't so bad, really. I was slightly dazed and ate a lot of soup. And the men stopped coming around for what seemed a couple of weeks, but it was hard to tell since their presence had been the factor that determined time. We stayed awhile, I guess. My body scabbed up, and I kept opening the wounds to draw out the salt water. I wanted some lasting memory of the night Mother fell in love with me again. I finally got the pockmark scar that I wanted above my left eye and then let myself heal. The whole scenario of the house on Third Street was all a bit complicated for Mother. She had found brief ecstasy, but failed to find romantic love, so she turned once again to loving me and anointing us with oil each night. Now she slept with me and played the Doobie Brothers, which was my favorite. Some song called "Black Water." Well I built me a raft and it's ready to float. . . She dreamt of the bugs crawling in between the cracks in the window frame. With a big black platform shoe she beat them until they blended in with the carpet. After she killed five, ten more appeared, and finally she made a decision to leave Upper Michigan; but she had already been bitten and didn't even know it. And we slept a long time while the arm of the record player kept lifting and settling the needle into a groove again and again.

And then we moved. ✧

City Storms

Jeffrey M. Bockman

1.

A thunderstorm in New York is magical. The city, once the province
of throngs of people—tattered or nattily attired, intent on their business
or pleasures, flitting through film-projector flickerings of light and dark
as the sun alternately strikes through the spaces between skyscrapers and
is then blocked out again, from block to block and one side of the street
to the other—becomes in an instant almost emptied as the day goes from
an expansive brightness, where, despite the buildings, the sky seems not
something all about us but something way above, to a silvery haze and
then an enveloping, palpable black. Umbrella sellers once from diverse
foreign lands, uprooted by dire events or simply seeking the mythical
land of promise, and now rooted here in this asphalt topsoil, spring up
from nowhere hawking their wares. Where does everyone go in that
instant—shopping, eating, sipping coffee? The stores and restaurants
and cafes never seem suddenly overstuffed, and surely most people are
many blocks, neighborhoods, boroughs, if not cities from home.

2.

Strange things then begin to happen.

I have seen the central concrete-dry fountain in Washington Square
Park, once an expanse for jugglers and other tourist-pleasers, become a
shimmering, phosphorescent pool, where by the water's dim light I have
watched entranced as intrepid children—somehow out in the storm
while their parents huddle for comfort in unknown retreats and their
nannies or teachers have all fallen into thunderstruck stupors, allowing
them to sneak out in their raincoats on special missions—tossed balls
across to each other across this small inland sea, or set adrift on these
sparkling waves odd wooden boats with slanted tops for the rain to run off.

I have seen a small shop off Minetta Lane, where I would sometimes
buy a Coke or a beer, or in my youth rolling papers, suddenly unfold, like
one of those pop-up cards that open up into a miniature replica of a
Victorian house. Where once the tiny space could barely fit three people,
now there were hallways leading to more rooms and an upstairs accessed
via a rickety ladder, and a hidden space behind a bookshelf that of course
was never there before because they didn't sell books. And while the
front anteroom, as it had now become, was still stuffed with junk food
and cigarettes and condoms and all the other quick-fix items, these other
rooms displayed an assortment of oddities: one room housed old archeo-
logical finds labeled from their city blocks, for example "Fragments of

Household Items, 18th Street and 5th Avenue" or "Gambling dice, Lafeyette and Bond." Another room held old recipe books, how to make apple champagne or birch wine, nestled amidst remedies for chilblains and homemade poisoned fly paper, amidst cinnamon ink and belladonna eyeliner and silver-impregnated photographic-capable pottery clay. Behind the bookshelf was a large room filled with old mechanical toys and turn of the century arcade games. I never even had time to explore all the alcoves and backrooms because the thunderstorms never lasted long enough, and as the sound of the storm faded from the shop, the rooms seemed to collapse upon themselves until I would find myself once again merely browsing amidst the few magazines.

3.

There is a hushed camaraderie that arises with the daytime storm. The boisterousness of the noon lunch hour, with its preening and bragging and strutting and flirting and scurrying and gorging and chattering and yelling all giving way to a subdued fellowship of whispering and sipping and page-turning and drowsing and scribbling and rustling and breathing. Time slows, the waiters slow, the steam rising from the coffee cups slows and looks like cartoons of steam rising from coffee cups. I have seen a woman read all of Proust over one cappuccino. I have seen a man asleep over his newspaper waking refreshed from his eight hours compressed into half an hour of thunder-syncopated dreams (my watch goes from noon until eight p.m., only to instantaneously reset to twelve thirty as he stirred and stretched and returned to perusing his paper).

4.

In the play of lightning and thunder and torrents of rain sometimes down but often sideways and even up, not just time but also space plays games, twisting and inverting the laws of geometry and physics. In thunderstorms taking place in simultaneously enshrouded capitals, passageways open up allowing one to walk between Bloomsbury and Sheridan Square, between the Jardins des Plantes and the New York Public Library, between the Trevi Fountain and Macy's, between Golden Gate Park and the Frick. For the duration of the weather's quirky machinations, one can enjoy a quick pint of ale or some Ghirardelli chocolate or a citron pressé or an egg cream. It is also possible to flit from Downtown to Uptown, from Eastside to Westside, without the hassle of bus or subway or taxi. The only problem is one of controlling one's destination—one can't. I have stepped into a telephone booth in the Peninsula Hotel dripping with rain, only to emerge in the sawdust at Chumley's, and dry at that. I have left the Mission Café with an espresso in hand, thinking the downpour had ceased, and as I passed onto the sidewalk of what I expected to be Second Avenue found myself instead beneath the torrential skyfall in front of Le Pain Quotidien on Madison and Eighty-fourth. This probably doesn't happen to everyone, and certainly not everyone would appreciate the magical displacement.

5.

But perhaps the most magical of all is to sit inside my apartment. The streetlamps flicker on; I turn off the lights and stereo. The streets are empty save for the occasional person running with a *Times* or a *Newsday* over their head. I sit atop the bed and look at the three windows on my corner. The city is silent except for the rain and the thunder and the few taxis. The pigeons have disappeared. The church spires are a red brick against the black clouds. Sometimes the air goes greenish, like an aquarium, or yellow-black, like a bruise. If the wind is wild enough, the windows get washed of the accumulated weeks or months of city dust. I sit and I watch, in an isolation not lonely or sad but with a certain cozy melancholy, like being inside a poem. ✧

CRITICISM

POST ROAD

On the Aesthetic Agenda of the Antiwar Movement

Lori Cole

photographs by Lori Cole

While avenues for sanctioned political resistance are being increasingly restricted by the federal government, the political left has been using the irreverent, innovative tactics of the visual to express fury and garner support for the antiwar movement. Artists can get away with a lot—blasphemy, controversy, confrontation—in the name of cultural expression. Since patronage and institutional support for work meant to spark debate can be seen as neutralizing and reifying, activist artists have escaped political inefficacy by directing their skills, funding, and their knack for getting attention to pressing political issues, taking the street as their venue and the general public as their audience. Likewise, protesters apply high art aesthetics to do-it-yourself methods to streamline their messages into slogans, express themselves through images, and harness a playful energy for their cause. The use of street stencils, posters, and protest paraphernalia that developed around the recent antiwar movement gestures towards '6os-era traditions of artistic resistance and reinvigorates them for a fresh political purpose. Such visual production also redirects earlier activist public art movements of the '8os and '90s that focused on identity or community-based issues towards new collective action. The diverse agendas, complex affiliations, and conflicting identifications of demonstrators serve as the fiercest resistance to recent government setbacks by embodying a democratic public space that is characterized by difference and strengthened by debate.

A scruffy-haired teenager carries an orange sign proclaiming "War is terrorism" alongside an old man in a baseball cap with a sheet of notebook paper reading "Another veteran for peace." Members of a socialist organization wield enormous "No Blood for Oil" signs depicting a mournful girl in pigtails. A middle-aged woman carries an "Axis of Weasels" picture complete with caricatures of Cheney, Bush, and Rumsfeld. Some posters simply state "International Criminal Court," while others colorfully depict what "Bush's empty warhead" looks like. From the hastily scribbled to the mass produced, these posters and signs play on feelings of rage, incredulity, helplessness, and empowerment. They also serve as counter-proclamations to repressive government policy and unilateral military strikes, suggesting alternatives that range from pleas for UN approval to anarchy. Activist ingenuity registers on the bodies of protesters as well: a man is draped toga-style in the American flag, a piece of duct tape covering his mouth, wearing a sign reading "Patriot Act." Another wears a Bush mask while juggling a toy globe with blood-covered hands. These colorful, cheaply made, and easily disseminated visual statements reveal not only what is at stake at these protests— protection of civil liberties, opposition to American imperialism—but also the grassroots diversity of political identifications at play in the broader peace movement. Such art serves as a counter-history to what is being expressed in official discourse. Protesters hope their posters appear in newspapers or on television, on buildings and in streets, as accessible visual reminders of a crowd's density, creativity, and fighting spirit.

Before there were antiwar posters, there were government-issued propaganda posters, intended to popularize American military objectives. The government rallied support for World War I with bright, recognizable posters because much of the American population was illiterate. Even after these conditions changed, the propagandistic poster, demanding military service, obedience, and economy, became associated with wars, and it continued to be a convenient tool for controlling subversive behavior ("Loose lips sink ships!") and encouraging economic investment in the government ("Buy war bonds!"). As a result, the Left considered the political poster a battleground for what images and slogans dominate the culture and what opinions get formed accordingly. This practice continues: in a neat inversion of the Uncle Sam recruitment poster ("I want YOU!"), a crippled post-Vietnam Uncle Sam screams, "I want OUT!" in a 1970s street protest poster[1]. In our media-saturated culture, such anti-establishment posters retain their power by allowing for quick recognition and then an inversion of expectations for the viewer.

Advertisements, billboards, street signs, graffiti—both institutionally generated and independent, oppositional, visual texts—clutter the walls and sidewalks of city streets, vying for the public's attention. Textual site-specific street art has to intervene in these spaces, making itself legible and provocative amidst the multiplicity of urban languages. While these textual responses range in content and context, most adopt the formal block lettering of an ad or billboard. Starting in 1977, artist Jenny Holzer

---

[1] *"Propaganda" exhibition at the Chisholm Gallery, 55 W 17 St. 6th Fl. NYC 10011.*

postered buildings with what she called "Truisms," written observations on the allocation of wealth and influence, such as "Abuse of power should come as no surprise." Using segments of time purchased by the Public Art Fund on a spectacolor board in Times Square in 1982, Holzer drew attention to political and social inequalities through slogans such as "It is man's fate to outsmart himself." Co-opting the language of advertising, in 1991 Barbara Kruger placed posters in bus shelters throughout New York City promoting awareness of women's political issues. Pictures of men screamed, "Help! . . . I've decided to enter politics. The campaign is going really well but I just found out I'm pregnant. What should I do?" By situating attention-grabbing messages in public spaces, artists can expose the inadequacies and discrimination that shape official discourse, thereby opening up spectacle to doubt, difference, and debate.

Since the 1960s, artists have been forming collectives to battle political issues both in and outside of the art world. A group called Artists Protest formed in 1965 to oppose the war in Vietnam, sponsoring "Angry Arts Week" in 1967, replete with a range of performances, actions, and rallies. Artists Poster Committee formed in 1969, as a subgroup of the Art Workers Coalition, to produce and distribute anti-Vietnam War posters. The successful non-profits Creative Time and the Public Art Fund began in the 1970s to fund alternative and often ephemeral public art projects, offering alternative means of production and distribution for art[2]. Merging political campaigning with artistic practice, artists participating in activist collectives such as Group Material, Guerilla Girls, ACT UP, and Political Art Documentation and Distribution (PAD/D) integrated well-honed slogans with graphic design to rally around issues such as homelessness, gentrification, discrimination, AIDS, American foreign and economic policies—and even art elitism. Group Material dissected the term "democracy" in one of their poster campaigns. PAD/D, as described by one of its founding members, Lucy Lippard, "began in 1979 as an archive of socially concerned art to combat the suppression and amnesia about activist art internationally and almost immediately became an activist organization as well."[3] Such activist artists drew attention to the exclusion of minorities, women, and homosexuals from the established art world and to the interconnectedness of these different identity groups' continued rights struggles.

For artists hoping to change both the production and circulation of art and to incite public anger over political issues, the street serves as an ideal location for radical aesthetic interventions. As the site of public interaction, confrontation, and collaboration, the street functions as a microcosm of local urban democratic experience, and thus as a location in which to model political theories through applied artistic practice.

[2] *Ault, Julie.* Alternative Art New York: 1965-1985. *Minneapolis, Minnesota: Minnesota UP, 2002.*

[3] *Lippard, Lucy, "Biting the Hand: Artists and Museums in New York Since 1969."* Alternative Art New York: 1965-1985. *Ed. Julie Ault. Minneapolis, Minnesota: Minnesota U P, 2002; 104-5.*

While certain streets, marked for "redevelopment" or "aestheticization" projects, are indeed socially stratified, many public streets serve as a theater for various conflicting interests, where a mixing of ethnicities, classes, and ideas often occurs. Michel de Certeau's "Walking in the City" focuses on the opportunities the city offers to subvert official order: "Beneath the discourses that ideologize the city, the ruses and combinations of powers that have no readable identity proliferate."[4] By inscribing words onto architecture, by subverting the space of the advertisement, public artists try to dismantle dominant political ideology through popular, visual instruments of communication. Walking in the city is part of "inventing" space, according to de Certeau, displacing the imposed order and inserting yourself within a re-signified order: "The surface of this order is everywhere punched and torn open by ellipses, drifts, and leaks of meaning: it is a sieve-order," he explains.[5] By opening up spaces for dissent, artists force viewers to question the demands made by billboards and advertisements, as well as their own complacency as passive consumers of city-mandated texts.

Political stickers, graffiti, and posters signal to a wide audience that there exist alternative modes of political influence and avenues for debate. Many demonstrators use signs and slogans to include themselves in and also to invite others into a larger framework of accepted rhetoric. This strain of the antiwar movement produces phrases such as "Peace is Patriotic" and "Support the Troops, Bring Them Home." Other approaches employ a lighthearted sarcasm to cope with a sense of exclusion from national decisions. *Onion* newspaper headlines such as "Dead Iraqi Would Have Loved Democracy" are winks to the antiwar movement, acknowledging the hypocrisy of the government with laughter.[6] Such inversion, invention, and insertion of mockery into the art produced by those involved in the antiwar movement uses playfulness to confront frightening realities. Self-critique, laughter, and exuberance invigorate crowds, offering relief amidst depressing headlines and neglect from a radically conservative administration. Aesthetic playfulness—the brightly colored poster board, the obscenities, the distorted presidential portraits, the costuming and fanfare—infuses every moment of a protest, allowing the Left to celebrate its ingenuity without having to sacrifice its ideals. It is at this intersection of aesthetics and activism that I would like to situate the public sphere created by recent demonstrations: at the forefront of new forms of debate, in confusion and celebration, in anger and in pride.

Idealized as a spatial location, a discursive site, or a mass of people, the "public" has indelibly inscribed itself on the political imagination. The idea of "public consensus" is seductive, marketable. After all, isn't the demo-

---

[4] de Certeau, Michel. "Walking in the City." *The Practice of Everyday Life. Trans. Steven F. Rendall.* Berkeley: University of California Press, 1984; 158.

[5] de Certeau, 160.

[6] "Dead Iraqi Would Have Loved Democracy." The Onion, 39:11, March 26 2003.

cratic political promise to represent and serve the public? By fashioning their own definitions of what constitutes the public, ideologues of all political persuasions lay claim to this term, touting their political agendas as universally beneficial and ethically sound. Protesters at this past year's demonstrations sought to destroy the illusion of "public" consensus through their actions.[7] Even the *New York Times* recognizes the effectiveness of this approach:

> The fracturing of the Western alliance over Iraq and the huge antiwar demonstrations around the world this weekend are reminders that there may still be two superpowers on the planet: the United States and world public opinion. In his campaign to disarm Iraq, by war if necessary, President Bush appears to be eyeball to eyeball with a tenacious new adversary: millions of people who flooded the streets of New York and dozens of other world cities to say they are against war based on the evidence at hand.[8]

Bush's war for approval was played out in terms of public opinion, a vague term informed by polls, not by protests. "Public opinion" operates according to the logic of the public as an idealized, homogenous, universal body, or as a series of pluralistic subjects with identical collective concerns. The federal administration seeks to enact a vision of the public that is carefully scripted, structured, and exclusive. Meanwhile the Left idealizes its own version of the public: one that questions the rhetoric of community and subjectivity. "Social space is produced and structured by conflict," art historian Rosalyn Deutsche explains—and it is at these points of conflict or contiguity that similarities between political projects are recognized and that real democratic debate occurs.[9] By being self-conscious about its construction of a counter-discourse of the public, critical public art and activism can model and initiate alternate visions of the public. The posters activists devised in the antiwar protests this year drew attention to the condition of conflict, serving collectively as a site for sustained confrontation. It is through questioning governmental declarations and media-generated texts, and through critically re-examining relationships between people of varying socioeconomic and ethnic backgrounds and political interests that one can begin to contest the idea of a uniform public. For demonstrators, laying claim to a broad and representative constituency of Americans became the crucial definition of "the public," and by extension, public opinion.

The public sphere has long been a rhetorical space available for the disenfranchised to potentially influence government policy. Political

---

7 *Clementson, Lynette. "Threats and Responses: Rally; Thousands Converge in Capital to Protest Plans for War."* New York Times, *January 19, 2003.*

8 *Tyler, Patrick E. "Threats and Responses: News Analysis; A New Power in the Streets."* New York Times, *February 17, 2003..*

9 *"Deutsche, Roslyn. Evictions. Cambridge, MA: MIT Press, 1996; xxiv.*

theorist Jürgen Habermas defines the public sphere as an arena between the state and society where problems of public welfare are debated in an atmosphere free of restrictions and characterized by "rational" discourse. "A portion of the public sphere comes into being in every conversation in which private individuals assemble to form a public body," Habermas argues.[10] Casual, friendly conversations as well as the more fiery political arguments that arise at protests formally adhere to this Habermasian model. As Habermas aptly points out, public opinion is produced by the willful participation of constituents, keen on conserving their right to criticize and control the behavior of their government. However, he recognizes that such a promise of political influence is impossible to realize in the climate of late capitalism, when private interests influence decision-making and control communication.

Though antiwar demonstrators have not had their opinions represented in Congress and have not been acknowledged by government assessors of public opinion, they do serve as a version of the public themselves, in their boas and berets, with their strollers and megaphones. Many of the cries heard at recent protests, as frustration mounts, concern the nature of democracy. Though many participants cannot resolve their positions on specific political issues, all recognize that there should at least be a debate, and that debate is fundamental to democratic decision-making structures. "Whose streets? Our streets," as well as "This is what democracy looks like," were repeated as policemen barricaded streets, arrested activists, and forced protesters onto sidewalks at the February 15, 2003, rally in New York City. By claiming democracy, protesters suggest that their ranks are composed of people with diverse political agendas and backgrounds, as opposed to the homogenous public referred to by government pollsters, or the "focus group" President Bush referred to as a way of dismissing the internationally coordinated large-scale February 15 protests.

Political theorist Chantal Mouffe locates political agency in the kinds of alliances that are formed between disparate political groups. While Mouffe, like Habermas, believes that debate is fundamental to a productive public sphere, she disagrees with Habermas that such a debate occurs according to the terms of rational discourse, which would end in consensus, a unified public opinion that can then inform state decisions. Rather, she argues, individuals adopt multiple, contradictory, and discursively constructed subject positions. Speakers used the podium at the Washington and New York rallies to draw a sympathetic audience's attention to causes ranging from gender discrimination to education policies. Participants also raised awareness of personal issues, but subsumed them under the larger rhetoric and goal of the antiwar movement: peaceful reconciliation, diplomatic dialogue, and recognition of other nations'

---

[10] *Habermas, Jürgen, "The Public Sphere: An Encyclopedia Article (1964)."* New German Critique *(Fall 1974) 49.*

interests and concerns. Therefore, at protests, in addition to declarations of democracy, one overheard slogans like "Money for jobs, not for oil," and "Build schools, not bombs." Further optimistic agendas were disclosed: rather than just denouncing Bush, people rallied for alternate political candidates. Gray-haired women with feathered boas marched proudly and sang, '60s-era peace songs behind a large "Code Pink, Women's Pre-Emptive Strike for Peace" banner. Protesters identified themselves as businessmen, parents, Yale graduates, veterans, and Texans, so as not to be absorbed by an amorphous "movement" or dismissed as "liberal college students."

Mouffe argues that a person who recognizes the slippages between his or her own political identifications—based on national origin, ethnicity, race, class or gender—will, by extension, also recognize the necessity to align him or herself with other disadvantaged individuals and groups seeking political and economic equality, especially those in close social proximity. Some protests held in specific racial strongholds emphasized particular counter-agendas to that of war, such as the Black Radical Congress youth rally in Harlem. While the multiplicity of issues raised at protests, from the first one in Washington in October through the March 22 rally in New York, do indicate the government's ever-growing neglect of its constituents' interests, it also distracts protesters and media alike from the urgency of the antiwar message. Street demonstrations of this nature therefore did represent a kind of democratic process. A kaleidoscope of opinions, personal fury over a spectrum of issues, indecisiveness, extremist visions, and utopic possibilities: a gathering of incongruent masses, poised alongside each other, cheering and shouting. The efficacy of such marches was hard to tally in numbers or in media coverage, and usually took the form of personal and interpersonal transformation: a bright-eyed old gentleman recounting stories of civil rights marches in Washington to girls leading their first protest chants; a family waving peace signs from a Fifth Avenue window.

Artists model this democratic version of the public sphere and implement it on a small scale by creating alternative networks for disseminating information that question the national discourse. From the Theaters Against the War staging of the ancient Greek antiwar play *Lysistrata*, in fifty-nine different countries, to the "Poems Not Fit for the White House" reading at Lincoln Center, to a show at the Chisholm Gallery juxtaposing government-sponsored war propaganda posters with responses created by the Left, a broad swath of the art world uses their networks to support the antiwar movement.[11] There exist literally hundreds of online sources for antiwar posters, such as the "Another Poster for Peace" web site, whose slogan is "copyright-free art for public use," encouraging sharing resources for the purposes of solidarity and refuting the autonomy or ownership of art. Poster art facilitates the move-

---

[11] West, Debra, "No Sex as Antiwar Protest? What Sex?" New York Times, March 9 2003.

ment's visibility in newspapers, on television, and to passersby on the street. Such visual production remains as one of the few public outlets available for debate. The posters "Fuck Bush- It Feels Good" and "War is Unhealthy for Children and Other Living Things," while seemingly incongruous, inhabit the same stretch of Fifth Avenue in New York City or the Mall in Washington, mimicking the daily mixture of cultures in urban street life and the wide constituency that begs representation at the level of government.

Eager to construct a counter-history to the one being advocated by the government, protesters assert their presence through visual reminders: buttons seen in passing on coats and purses, graffiti stenciled on a city sidewalk. Protesters also infiltrate dominant spaces of communication, such as billboards or newspapers, and provide alternative venues for debate— at community centers, through independent media outlets, and on the street. Recent antiwar demonstrations have proved that there is no fixed political identity of the Left, and that any such vision of "the public"—even one against the Iraq war—is unproductive. Nor is there a single utopic vision of the future. If anything, the spate of recent antiwar protests demonstrate that "the public square has to be reinvented again and again . . . anyone with experience of the Left knows that those unhappy with an existing critical space will feel free to invent new ones, more receptive to their needs. There is no set formula for the dialectic of institutionalization and fluidity which defines the idea of the public square."[12] Politically and publicly minded artists help to subvert the neutralizing tactics of a government's tacit dismissal of their dissent and to instigate this reinvention.

The fluid, inclusive DIY culture that produces and inseminates clever, direct, and inexpensive art encourages others to visually render and promote their own politics. Such aesthetic material is in dialogue with more established socially minded artistic practices, such as the large-scale public art projects of Kruger, Holzer, and Group Material. Artists can use their influence as recognized cultural producers to persistently poke holes in the official discourse, allowing room for a multiplicity of subject-positions to filter through. The DIY aesthetic of the antiwar movement's artistic production is free form, contradictory, and open to working with artists and activists alike to disseminate a message of peaceful coexistence. Yet the beginnings of a broad-based coalition movement emerged as participation at protests increased throughout the year and protesters unified through internationally consistent slogans, posters, and practices. With involvement from a range of politically identified subgroups, the antiwar movement creates an atmosphere of sustained debate at protests, embodying the model of democracy it seeks to enact. These conversations and confrontations will lead to further social engagement, applying old forms of political and artistic intervention to new purposes and developing aesthetic tactics for an ever-evolving public sphere. ✧

---

[12] *Hirschkop, Ken, "The Public Square as Public Sphere."* Mikhail Bakhtin: An Aesthetic for Democracy. *New York: Oxford UP, 1999; 271*

ART

POST ROAD

Mary Armstrong: Paintings

Introduction by Claude Cernuschi

The theme of nature is crucial to the development of Mary Armstrong's imagery. Whether in the form of a tree, a seascape, a rock, a bird, a flower, or an abstracted cluster of forms throbbing and pulsating with the vibrancy of a human heart, the force and potency of the natural dimension runs throughout the entire range of the paintings illustrated here.

In spite of this general unity of purpose, there is also great diversity. Some paintings, such as the members of the *Cold, Clear, Light* series conform to the conventional landscape format. The presence of a horizon line provides both an architectonic anchor for the compositions and a clear frame of reference for the spectator to interpret the scenes. It also sets up a tension between the permanence of the horizon line and the impermanence of all natural manifestations that pass before it: the ephemeral quality of light, the movement of the water, the tree in bloom, or even the illusory stability of the rocks, themselves doomed to be eroded by the passage of time. The changing and the changeless, time and place, death and life, are all evoked by means of Armstrong's landscapes.

The presence of the tree in *Cold, Clear, Light # 1* is also reminiscent of the way trees were used by Romantic landscape artists as surrogate individuals, as natural forms displaying as much anthropomorphic qualities and psychological presence as a human portrait. Yet the contrast between the verticality of the tree and horizontality of the earth gives way in *Cold, Clear, Light # 4* to an overpowering sense of connection, rather than contrast, between natural forms. As our eyes are being led gradually from one part of the composition to the other, air, earth, water tend to merge in a continuity of motion where the perpetual and general energy—rather than the specific manifestations—of nature tends to emerge in sharper relief.

The same could be said of the *Heartbeat* series, where a blooming flower, a pulsating form, or a winged bird stand as the kernel of a flowing universe in constant motion. In this way, the rhythmic beating of the heart becomes a way of drawing a connection between humanity and nature, between the inside and the outside, between the life of a single individual and the life force of the cosmos as a whole. But this beating motion can suggest struggle as well as connection. Just as the tree or the rocks in the *Cold, Clear, Light* series could evoke the fragility of life and the passage of time, the heart and the bird begin to appear highly vulnerable within the very sublime immensity of

the cosmic rhythms of which they are a part. The grander motion and energy of nature is stronger than any single animal or person, and, as a result, human beings and animals equally run the risk of being overwhelmed, even destroyed by the scale of the forces at work all around them. The darker forms in Armstrong's work thus also look ominous, as if a dire, unending struggle is taking place between life and death, light and the absence of light. ✧

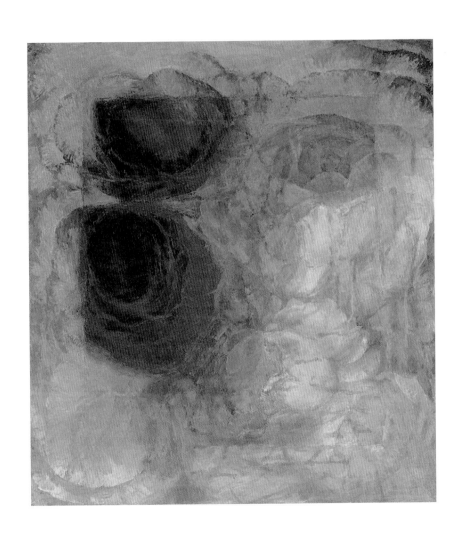

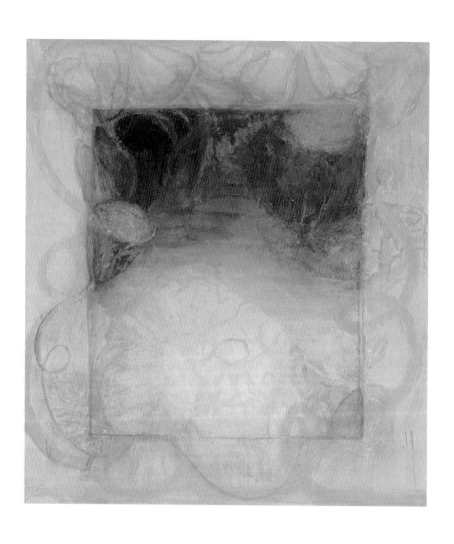

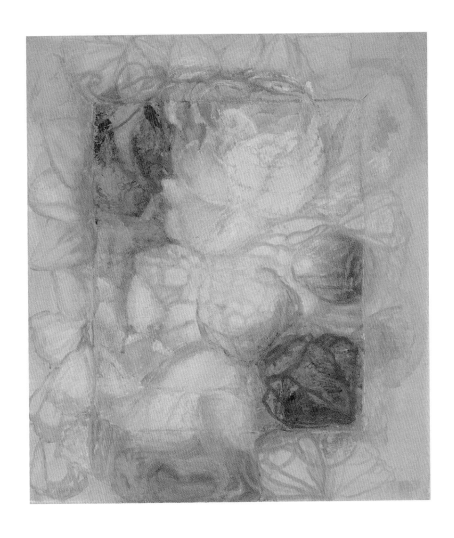

Stoney Conley: Paintings

Introduction by Claude Cernuschi

Stoney Conley's pieces illustrated here comprise the building blocks for a series. They are all related visually and, iconographically, and contain a strong autobiographical component. In particular, the works are visual responses to the tragic passing of both the artist's parents within a remarkably short span of time. Given that Conley's mother was a gardener, the ubiquity of the flower in this series functions, specifically, as a metonym for the deceased parent and for her love of living and growing things. But the presence of the flower, depicted here in various states of blooming and fading, is also more generally symbolic (ever since 17th-century Dutch still-life painting) of the brevity and fragility of human life. In these works, therefore, flowers play a complex dual role. Firstly, they function as a memorial to a particular individual—to that individual's love of life and positive contribution to her environment—and, secondly, as a reference to the long tradition in art history of employing flowers to convey the inescapable passing of time.

The dark colors, reductive simplicity, and the absence of any distracting details in this series also accentuate the tragic mood of the individual pieces. As does the presence of the moon, which was full the night of Conley's mother's passing, and which hovers over the flowers, partly as a physical, celestial body, and partly as some nearly supernatural, metaphysical reference to the possibility of an afterlife. Again, Conley's work recalls prototypes in the history of art where celestial objects—suns, moons, or stars—were also used to convey a more subjective, contemplative, even philosophical mood. In the works of Romantic artists such as Caspar David Friedrich or Post-Impressionists such as Vincent van Gogh, heavenly spheres were frequently meant to represent a pantheistic connection with nature, as well as to communicate the potential of spiritual transcendence within the confines of an otherwise limited and material world. In Conley's work, here, the position of the flower below and of the moon above play out a similarly delicate but equally portentous dialectic.

Conley, moreover, heightens the sense of the moon's evocative power by allowing it to peer through the diaphanous veil of a hovering white cloud, which both reveals as well as obscures the presence of, and light emitted by, this elusive sphere. This intricate play between light and dark, presence and absence, revelation and obfuscation, thus reinforces both the specificity of the mood and of the commemorative event that these pieces are meant to evoke. It is no less important to  mention that there is also a congruity between meaning and form in many of Conley's works—especially *Ghost Flower*. The form of the flower is often outlined by means of a process of scraping away, allowing the ground or underpainting to show through. This is especially apposite given that the pieces are about absence and the passing away of all things terrestrial. ✧

CONLEY

Mary Armstrong: Paintings

Cold, Clear, Light #4, Oil on panel, 24" x 22", 2002

Heart Beat #4, Oil on panel, 24" x 22", 2002

Cold, Clear, Light #1, Oil on panel, 20" x 18", 2002

Heart Beat #2, Oil on panel, 24" x 22", 2002

Untitled #3, Oil on panel, 20" x 18", 2002

Untitled #2, Oil on panel, 20" x 18", 2002

Heart Beat #3, Oil on panel, 24" x 20", 2002

Stoney Conley: Paintings

Ghost Flower, Oil on canvas, 20" x 20", 2001

Ghost Malva, Oil on canvas, 24" x 20", 2002

Spirit Flower: Peonie, Oil on canvas, 20" x 16", 2002

Spirit Malva, Oil on canvas, 20" x 16", 2002

Spirit Flower: Rhodadendrum, Oil on canvas, 16" x 12", 2002

Spirit Rhodadendrum, Oil on canvas, 24" x 20", 2002

Night Blooming Memory, Oil on canvas, 24" x 20", 2001

FICTION

POST ROAD

Dream Children

Edith Pearlman

Willa found the first portrait on a July evening while she was straightening her room. She had invited the two older boys to play there before bedtime, and the floor was strewn with chessmen and Othello counters. She picked up these fragments and put them where they belonged: in the next-to-lowest drawer of a scarred, ivory-knobbed chest—an architect's chest, the mother had told her—that stood under the window. Willa's own blouses and underwear lay in the shallow upper drawers. The chest and a lamp and a bed—a bed not quite long enough; she often slept on the floor—were the only furnishings in this narrow room behind the kitchen; but the other rooms didn't have much in them either. In her country there was a TV in every village bar, and in the Capital City even the poorest family owned a set. But in this New York apartment—none. "We don't like to watch, we don't want the children to watch," said the mother that first day, looking up anxiously at tall Willa. "But if you wish . . . "

"No, Ma'am."

"No 'Ma'am' please," the mother cried.

"No Ma'am please," Willa repeated.

"No, no, I mean, do call us by our first names, Sylvie . . . "

"Yes, Ma'am," Willa said.

" . . . and Jack."

The bottom drawer in the architect's chest was stuck. Every night she caressed the knobs as if to fool them, dark fingers soothing the ivory, and then gave a single sudden yank. Tonight the thing slid out at last. In the drawer were some large, deckled drawing papers, face down. She picked up the top one and turned it over.

It was a pencil and watercolor portrait of a little boy. The left side of the child's face bulged like a potato, a blue and purple potato. It wasn't swollen because someone had smacked him, wasn't bruised either; the worst smack couldn't do that; he had been born that way. The eye above the bulging cheek seemed okay. The right side of the face was ordinary. The lower lip was a rubbery ledge, bigger on the left than on the right. The upper lip almost met the lower lip on the big side of the face and didn't meet it at all on the other side. Spittle, she could see it, a few curly lines.

Boy's costume was like Pinocchio's: shorts, a honey-colored vest, a shirt, knee socks. The black hair was thick and neatly parted. Somebody was taking care of him. He carried a toy boat. There was a friendly dog at his feet, exactly the color of the vest.

The portrait was signed with a date—five years ago—and initials, J. L. The father's imagining, then.

Willa put Boy back in the drawer. She went into the living room. They liked her to join them there, just as they liked her to eat with them. They worried about everything—traffic, poisons in food, mosquitoes, whether she was happy.

Dr. Gurevich from across the street was talking, her eyes huge in her square face. "I will bar the door," she rasped. "I will lie down in front of the bulldozer." She leaned forward. "I will drill their evil skulls."

Then she leaned back, as if to get away from her own popping eyes. Maybe she had the goiter. She wore her gray hair in a bun.

The father said, "I heard of a group practice, three men on East Twelfth Street. They're looking for a fourth, and they'd prefer a woman."

"East Twelfth Street?" Dr. Gurevich sat up straight again. "I belong here, on West Eighty-fourth Street. The city has given me no satisfaction," she added.

"The firm who owns your building hasn't broken any laws," the father said. "I looked into it, remember?"

Dr. Gurevich was being evicted from her narrow building across the street. She was a dentist, and lived and worked in her second-floor apartment. Willa had been brought to see it one day in June by the ten-year-old, who planned to be a dentist himself. Patients sat on a chair in a bay window. "See, Willa, this would be a dining room for a regular person," the boy explained. He climbed into the chair. "Dr. Gurevich doesn't require a dining room," he said, opening his mouth and baring his teeth. Then he said, "Wider, please. She eats her soups wherever she likes—sometimes on the fire escape. Spit, please."

A firm had bought Dr. Gurevich's house and the one next door, and sent notices that condominiums were to be built. The current occupants must leave by July 1st.

Willa had watched July 1st come. She watched it go. The other tenants left. The dentist remained, along with the janitor, who lived in the basement. There wasn't much work for him in the building, so he planted vegetables and fruits in the deserted back garden. Raspberries were just emerging.

"You could plant squash," said Willa.

"We won't last until squash," he told her.

But tonight, Dr. Gurevich, raging in their living room, looked as if she would last forever.

There was a cheep from the end of the hall. The cheep came again, then again, then a rapid twittering of sounds.

Willa got up and walked down the long hall and went into the darkened bedroom. The five-year-old slumbered spread-eagled on his parents' bed. She rested her palm briefly on his back. His bony face lay in profile on the pillow. The three oldest boys resembled the mother—sharp features, long mouths, narrow intelligent eyes. The little fat fourth looked like the father. "Each one starts out looking like Jack," the mother had mentioned, and the father laughed: "All babies look like me."

Willa bent down to the cradle and slid her hands under the newest soul. Her fingers found a place beneath his head and her thumbs hooked around his moist armpits and she swung him up onto her shoulder. This always satisfied him for a while; he slept again, his nose against her neck, pressing the pulse there, life to life.

She brought him to the changing table that was wedged between sink and tub in the apartment's bathroom. The floor tiles were chipped, but there was a stained-glass window featuring a tall robed red-headed figure. "After Burne-Jones," the mother had bewilderingly said when she was showing Willa around. The mother was a part-time professor. The father was an engineer.

Willa changed the baby. He opened his eyes and stared at her. She carried him into the living room and handed him first to the dentist, who pressed him against her dress; and then to the father, who laid the child on his own wide thighs and stared at him as if to memorize the eyelids, the lips, the damp folds on the neck; and then to the mother, who said "Thank you, Willa." The mother released her firm little breast from her shirt; milk was already spurting.

"What a warm night," the dentist said.

"Warm," said the father serenely. "Warm?" he repeated with a nervous twitch of his cheek, as if he sensed a hurricane.

"Warm, sir," said Willa. That nightmare child in the bottom drawer —it was like having a secret family.

The baby suckled. The father and the dentist and Willa silently watched. They might have been under water; they might have been floating on the surface of a pond; they might have been sitting on lily pads like the illustrations in the favorite book of the second boy, the eight-year-old—a textbook about frogs.

The mother shifted the baby to the other breast. "Good night," said Dr. Gurevich. She let herself out and walked down the three flights and crossed the street.

A week later, at five in the afternoon, Willa opened the drawer and looked at another picture.

Its subject seemed to be female—at least, the figure was wearing a smocked dress. There was trimming on the puffed sleeve; she could tell from the swift little circles that the trimming was lace. Fine lines on the slender hands represented wiry hairs; broader lines on cheeks and chin were hair, too. There was fur on the scalp. This creature's eyes were dull. Her nose was all nostrils. The upper lip was long, and the mouth stretched widely in a smile without happiness.

The date on Monkey-girl's portrait was eight years ago, and the paper was initialed with the father's two letters. If he were hers, Willa thought, she'd insist that he purge his bowels with bark, once a week if need be.

Willa came out of her room to find Dr. Gurevich in the kitchen, heating some of her own soup. "My electricity has been turned off," said the dentist. "The janitor is hooking it up again, to somebody else's line, please don't ask me how."

"All right," said Willa.

"Willa, Willa, what is to become of me?"

Back home this old woman would have been respected. She would not have been forced to work. People would have brought her stew and beer and smokes, and she would have sat on her porch and looked at the sea. "I have a . . . leaf," Willa said.

Dr. Gurevich was silent. Then: "Something I could roll?"

Willa nodded. "I can show you how."

The woman sniffed. "And will it find me a new apartment and a new office?"

"It will ease your spirits."

They exchanged a long look. "Please," said Dr. Gurevich.

All of Willa's herbs were in the third drawer from the bottom, above the chess pieces. Rolling took a few minutes. She left Dr. Gurevich smoking in the kitchen. She picked up the baby without waking him and went down to the curb to meet the day camp bus. How tanned they had become. The five-year-old buried his face in her belly—it was a long day for him. The ten-year-old trudged into the building, the eight-year-old at his heels.

Upstairs the boys crowded into the kitchen to help prepare the evening's baked rice and salad. Dr. Gurevich took her weed into the living room. There, dark and featureless against the window, she looked like Aunt Leona, who told the future. "You will be useful to the family in New York," Leona had promised. "They will be kind to you, in their way."

The father came home. The mother came home. The janitor rang the bell and called up through the intercom that Dr. Gurevich's electricity was on again. Dr. Gurevich, throwing Willa a sweet glance, left the apartment to join him.

Dr. Gurevich's water got turned off early one August morning. The janitor—no longer on salary but still occupying a room in the basement—said he could attach their pipes to another main, but not before nightfall. The dentist canceled that day's patients. She had fewer patients now than formerly, and those that came urged her to find new premises. "They think it's easy to pull up roots," she said. "You understand how hard it is, Willa."

Willa nodded. She was holding the five-year-old on her lap. He had begged to stay home from camp that day. So the dentist, the mother, the baby, Willa, and the five-year-old, all sat on the stoop of the family's apartment house and watched the empty brownstone next to Dr. Gurevich's house get wrecked. Neighborhood children who didn't go to day camp watched, too, and some of their mothers. The wrecking ball swung forwards and backwards, attacking the façade like a boxer. Stone and glass and wood and plaster crumpled at its touch. Debris piled up. Meanwhile an earthmover in back picked up the junk and deposited it into an enormous dumpster. A few scavengers hung around.

Willa, abruptly homesick, thought of her mother's little house on stilts, and the foaming sea, and her own three daughters in their school uniforms.

The building gradually collapsed. The debris mounted in its stead. By midafternoon the wrecking truck had driven off, leaving the busy earthmover to its work. The ice cream truck jingled down the street.

The mother took the baby upstairs for a bath. The five-year-old dozed in Willa's lap. The street got more crowded: cars, teenagers on skates, the knife grinder, a bicycle whose wide basket carried stacks of straw boaters. "Hats! Hats!" shouted the cyclist. When the camp bus came it couldn't pull up against the right curb and so it parked on the left. The children would have to step out into the street, Willa saw. The bus had its flashers on, but who knew? "Hold him, please," said Willa to Dr. Gurevich, transferring the five-year-old to the dentist. Willa went out into the middle of the street and stood beside the bus, staring down the impatient cars. Behind her back she heard the children crossing the street—her two, and some others from the building. The father rounded the corner from the subway, and he started to run, though it couldn't have been easy, he was so fat. "Where's Paul! I don't see Paul!" he yelled, and Willa pointed to the child on the dentist's lap, and the father stopped running and took off his seersucker jacket and mopped his face with it, though she had ironed all his handkerchiefs just yesterday.

That night she looked at the third picture. This one was a baby dressed only in a diaper, a baby of about a year, the age of toddling. This child would never toddle. Instead of legs he had flippers; instead of arms, flippers. His eyes had no pupils. His bare chest was like any white baby's: pink, the nipples suggested by rosy dots, so sweet, she wanted to kiss them.

The date on Seal Baby was ten years ago. There were no more drawings: just the three.

When the youngest started to run a fever, the mother gave him some liquid medicine, not aspirin. "We don't give aspirin to babies, Willa."

"We don't either, Ma'am."

"Ma'am again—oh, oh, oh."

"... Sylvie," Willa managed.

When the fever continued—down in the morning, up again in the afternoon, higher still at night—the parents brought him to the pediatrician's office. Willa and the boys did a jigsaw puzzle at home. Virus not bacteria, the pediatrician said; it will run its course. "But how long is its course?" moaned the father on the fourth day. "You never had such a high fever," he accused the eight-year-old, who burst into tears. "I am sorry, I am sorry," said the father, and he hugged his son.

At night the adults took turns tending the infant, sitting in the living room rocking chair. While the mother was rocking him, Willa slid into the kitchen. She carried a packet of the reddish powder Aunt Leona had pounded from various nuts. She boiled water and let the powder steep. By the time it was her turn to rock the baby, the tea had cooled. She poured it into a bottle and slipped the bottle into the pocket of her apron. She took the baby and sat down on the rocker. Exhausted from fretting, he fell asleep on her shoulder. She heard the mother stumble into the bedroom. The father came out; she heard him in the kitchen opening some contraption, a folding chair maybe . . . There was a full moon. Through the living room window Willa saw Dr. Gurevich and the janitor walking down the street, arm in arm.

Willa took the bottle from her apron. She shifted the baby to her lap and cradled him and stroked first his left cheek and then his right, and at last he opened his eyes and then his mouth and she inserted the nipple. Looking at her, he drank about two thirds of the bottle. She could feel the heat draining from his body, feel his breathing become slower, feel the rasp in his chest grow still. He slept again. He smiled in his comfortable sleep. She got up and carried him into the kitchen. The contraption she had heard was an easel. The father was working at a drawing, intently using the side of his pencil to create shadows . . .

"Jack."

He turned. "What! What!"

"The fever has broken."

He took the baby from her. He was not ashamed to cry. But when she stared at the drawing—only a head, this time, pointed ears and one eye missing and an open mouth, lipless—he gave an embarrassed snort. "It's like an amulet; it's to prevent catast ... " She touched his shoulder to show she understood. Then she moved to the sink and took the bottle from her pocket and unscrewed the nipple and tipped the thing, and the rest of the amber-colored potion poured out in front of his eyes and hers. ✧

Since It's You

Peter Brown

I might have married Charlemagne, if he weren't *so* black. If he weren't as old as my own dead father would have been. I was waiting tables at the Circle Hill seven days a week for two years already—at 23 it was my whole life—and I had depended too much on him. He had more authority than anyone I knew, and I relied more on him for some things than anyone else, like the way he wrapped himself in a big white apron after he fired up his grill in the morning and never took it off till quitting time. This way we all knew that when the apron came off, it was time to lock up. We all were careful to respect the manager, a nervous college kid named Raymond, but Charlemagne knew when it was time. When that apron came off, nothing Raymond nor any of the others said mattered: the kitchen and dining room were clean and it was time to go.

He was a head taller than Raymond, two heads taller than me. He was slender as a shortstop but not so limber anymore—sometimes on Sunday mornings when he came in, the kitchen was cold and he limped about in his apron till he warmed up. He kept to himself that first hour in a manner I never understood. I watched him as I came and went from the dining room, how he ignored us as the grill heated up; he stared at the headlines for a long time before he licked his thumb and began moving his fingers through his newspapers. Sometimes a queasy desire arose in me, from somewhere near my stomach—sometimes his hands and head seemed all wrong to me, all a touch too big for his slender frame, and for that I wanted him and despised him too, because I wanted him perfect. His hair was pure white around his ears, almost fake in its beauty, since the rest of his hair was like his skin, blacker than the night behind the stars.

After the breakfast rush, he was more at ease. His manner changed. It was rare that he laughed, but when he laughed you could hear it clear out in the dining room. He was less predictable. Two of the girls truly hated him—Alex and especially Annie. Every time we stepped out for a smoke, they rode the same miserable little carousel of talk, going round and round on the same vicious wheel. First Annie aimed her cigarette at Charlemagne's Cadillac and carried on about how he went off by himself during his breaks and paraded those three big chamois rags (with his jacket over that filthy apron!) and Windexed the chrome and hubcaps and polished the golden letters of El Dorado scripted on the trunk like it was a christened yacht.

"Just because Charlemagne's black and has a better car than you," said Cheryl.

"Nope, it ain't that," said Annie. "I don't care about that."

"Yes, you do."

"No, I do not." One day during all this, there was a nervous silence, and then Annie stared at me a long time before she reported a rumor that Charlemagne had a wife and three little girls in Haiti and that although he sent money for the first few years, he stopped after he got the loan for that car.

"That can't be so," I said.

"Oh, yes it can."

That was when I stomped my cigarette and went back in. I avoided him, but after lunch he was pleasant to me, he smiled at me and on towards dinner he even looked at me as if puzzled by something, and shook his head in a way that embarrassed and pleased me. He treated me like a child—I knew that when he pretended to disapprove it was his way of pointing to something else. He was the most intelligent person I knew, the way he stacked the papers in English and French next to the grill and read them from a distance while he worked, flipping the pages between orders. As he read he was always railing, whispering against us, the USA, that is, for something horribly cynical or unforgivably naive we were doing some place in the world I never heard of. Once when I ran by, he put this big spatula over his head as if it were a flyswatter and something small and alive was circling my face.

"You Americans," he whispered to me. "You have the Fly of Death sitting on your nose but you cannot see it because it is too close." Then he put his face close and wiggled his big fingers at me. "You see? Why won't you chase it away?" He bit his lip and waved the spatula over his head like he was winding up to smash the fly. When I tried to look at my nose and crossed my eyes, he laughed so loud Raymond ran back into the kitchen and told him the customers were wondering. Later Charlemagne winked at me; my nose felt funny for the rest of the day, like something tiny and ticklish kept landing on it; twice I ran to the bathroom and looked in the mirror.

Charlemagne was right, though, and I knew what he meant. Sometimes you don't even see what you see. Once when I was a little girl riding my bicycle on a Saturday afternoon and from all directions the sirens wailed louder than I'd have imagined any noise could be, a lazy tornado-shaped column of black smoke rose from the center of the next block, my block, where my house was. I had only that morning learned to ride and was flying down the sidewalks too fast and off the curbs. Mrs. Spinelli waved a dishrag from her porch and called me into her house. Everyone was suddenly running out onto the avenue toward my street. After they were all gone, a few minutes later, I watched Charlie Wilson through Mr. Spinelli's picture window, the one black kid who came around our neighborhood and who was always accused of stealing bicycles. He acted tough and I hated him, but now as I watched him run toward my house, his face was a gray color I'd never seen and his eyes were frightened. As stupid as it seems now, thinking back, I felt sorry for him.

But that was twenty years ago. Another example was how my ex-boyfriend Jimmy came home drunk after work every night for two years, whistling and repeating the crazy things that went on at the Pussy Cat Club and I never minded, since at least then he would talk to me and not be mad. I laughed at his stories about the dancers and the bouncers, and I listened, but there was always something more he wanted from me, something he could never ask for, something I never knew how to give. Then he hadn't gone to work in months before I noticed—as obvious as it was. I couldn't see he paid no bills, never changed his clothes, or how bad things had become until the night he came in more shit-faced than ever and for no reason went for me with a hammer and chased me screaming around the kitchen table and out into the living room and around the sofa back into the kitchen until a neighbor called the cops and they came and dragged his ass away.

He came around the restaurant one time after that and despite the fit he put on out by the register, Raymond was afraid to throw him out. Jimmy was shouting I owed him money and he wanted it right goddamn now and some of the customers had even left but Raymond, with a wave of his hand to Rachel, said no, don't call the cops. He didn't want cops coming here all the time. Everybody stay calm, said Raymond, and he put his hands in front of him and waved them, going around Jimmy in a circle, as if that would calm him. I went back into the kitchen, but I heard Raymond apologize to Jimmy and say this really had nothing to do with him or this restaurant and suggested he go around back and I would meet him there in the lot to figure it out. Of course I refused and then Raymond came in pleading with me to please go get rid of him.

Throughout this episode Charlemagne sat on the Lo-Melt pretending to read or getting up to flip a hamburger. Raymond pleaded and I shook my head and we went around and around until Charlemagne stood up and took down a pair of bread knives from the wall and pushed between Raymond and me and out the back door, giving it a slam. All the girls crowded around the door and I couldn't see, but I could hear him letting loose some high-volume voodoo (that's what Annie said it was), and that was far worse than police.

After that I moved into a little three-bedroom place with Annie and Cheryl above the post office in Wittstown and began to work seven days. Every day when Charlemagne came in to get ready for lunch he ignored me for a while and I ignored him too and then after he had his coffee and an order of cinnamon toast he came along and asked me why I was in such a bad mood. This quickly became our little ritual.

"I'm in a good mood," I said. "What in the hell's the matter with you?"

"I feel wonderful," he would answer and frown at me in a way that gave me a terrible pleasure. I was a little afraid of him now—Jimmy had never reappeared—and if you ask me, that only complicated and sweetened the excitement of Charlemagne. You find a way of trusting people (I always do at least) and in a place like Raymond's, by and large, the people who come and go are good. The customers pay their bills, they give a reasonable tip, they don't make much mess.

One day a couple came in that seemed as worthy of faith as anyone alive. They were the outdoorsy type, sunny and serious, dressed in big boots and wool pants and Patagonias, as if maybe they had just come in from rock climbing, though the he carried the baby in its car seat and put his finger over his lips and whispered to me for a booth where the two of them and the car seat could sit. She stood behind him, smiling at me as she finished looping her ponytail into a knot.

"You bet," I said. "Right this way."

Once they settled in, he carried their jackets over to the hooks and she leaned over that car seat and cooed into it, like she had just opened the pot of gold at the end of the rainbow. The baby was unusually well-behaved though, judging from what little I had seen of her: she was absolutely quiet. Alex, the only one of us who has kids, says she never loves hers like when they're asleep.

When the hubby came back he studied the menu, turning it over and over, reopening the flaps in search of something that I guess simply wasn't there. She wanted a hamburger and fries and he settled at last for a bowl of oatmeal and a fruit salad from the breakfast page.

"Coffees?" I said.

She said yes and he said no. I took more interest in them than most clients, at first because I saw them pull into the front and there was something sad about their old blue Volvo and then, when they came in, they looked so handsome and healthy I envied them. The father had the nervous authority you see in newly minted doctors and lawyers, people that have gone through some impossible exam and come out not wise and wealthy but on the straight road to wisdom and wealth. They may not know much about their professions just yet, but they sure as hell know more than the rest of us about everything. She looked nicer, like she had a sense of humor and the grace that comes from knowing you'll soon enough be rich and respectable even if your current Volvo has 130K on it and a hubcap gone.

He asked me if I had any green tea, and I said I wasn't a thousand percent sure but doubted it and he asked for OJ. The next time I came back they were holding hands across the table and the baby was as quiet as before. I gave her coffee and him juice and hesitated before I asked if I could have a peek at the child. The mother looked a little concerned, only a little though, like she didn't want her to wake up, but the dad said, "Without a doubt," and turned the blanket away.

"Oh!" I said and wanted to cry or scream or run. I wanted to call Raymond, but something stopped me. I was embarrassed, thinking something was horribly wrong, that the baby had some deformity or worse, and I not knowing what to say, I only said, "So precious!" I couldn't see what it was that seemed so familiar and so misarranged. Its nose was a little high and the lips as thin and stretched as one of those little red rubber bands, the eyes as if pasted shut with Elmer's glue and first I thought she must be some kind of newbie! But she was stiff as old snow, there was nothing good-looking about her.

"What d'you call her?" I said.

"Roxanne," said the husband and they both looked hopefully at the child.

"How old?" I said.

"Two months," they both smiled, both staring again into the car seat. I watched the father and saw what I hadn't seen before: he was the kind you dread. He moved his beautiful brown eyes too anxiously around the table and the big room, then back to the car seat and I expected him at any moment to make some gesture with his finger, a signal that I was now to go place the order. I always remembered or imagined my own dad had been something different, someone who performed somersaults in the snow and played the ukulele and insisted on pistachio ice cream for breakfast or, when Mom wasn't along, that a friendly pretty waitress should sit down with us.

At the wake, with his casket open and his head like a stone in the silk and his hands over his heart, I couldn't see who he had been, what I should have known about him, or that they both, mom and dad, were truly gone. They had sent me out in summer with my bicycle and money for me and my friends for when the Good Humor Man came around. They liked to have a drink or two and a little private time together on a Saturday afternoon, but when I got back I always found them in bed having a nap.

I knew this was different, I understood they were dead, that the smoke had killed them quickly while they were asleep, not the flames and so on and so forth, as everyone in the world explained to me, as if it needed explanation fifty-thousand times over, but what I couldn't see at the time and what no one explained to me was that they were gone from me forever. They were permanently absent, like Brian McGuiness, who drowned in Readington Pond the spring before, and the next day at lavatory time the custodian came and removed his desk from the classroom.

I wasn't so stupid I figured they would bring the coffins into my bedroom at Aunt Ruthie's, although when Daddy's coffin went down into the hole it was abruptly too clear they wouldn't, that there were so many feet of dirt and rocks and eventually even many miles of country road between me and him. Somehow I didn't even care so much, not till Mom was lowered down. Until then I hadn't seen what it was. Until then it had been kind of fine to be at Ruthie's because she let me have chocolate milk three meals a day.

Back in the kitchen Charlemagne was dipping a basket of fries. I said, "Charlemagne, you come out front a minute because I want you to have a look at this new baby."

He shook his head. He had two hamburgers and a grilled cheese working on the grill.

"I don't like to see no new baby," he said. "You go out there and go crazy over the baby all you want, but I just stay here and short-order until it's time to go and then I go, you see?"

"No, I don't mean I want you to come and just ogle the baby, but there's something worrying me about it, about the baby," I said, whispering because I didn't want the other girls involved. "I just need a confirmation because I'm getting confused and upset and want you to come see for yourself."

"No," he said and gave a very annoying little laugh.

"Charlemagne," I said. "Please? For me."

At last he turned and could see how worried I was. He said nothing and wiped his hands on his apron and looked into the vat and tossed the fries one time all very slowly as if to say, "Alright, I'll come along, but I will do it not a split second before I am good and ready." When he was done with his orders he even sat down and opened the French paper and only folded it when I came back in the kitchen and led him out to have a look.

"I hope you don't mind," I said, and sparkled cheerfully at the young lawyer or whatever he was. "I was telling my friend about your baby and he just had to come see!"

Charlemagne and the dad eyeballed each other with all the collegiality of a cat and a crow, neither of them believing what I just said and neither of them believing the other believed it. The mother of course whispered, "Harris, it's fine. She won't wake up."

She was right. The dad removed the cover and the baby did not wake up. Charlemagne stopped. I felt his whole body and his long legs just stop where he stood. Maybe his heart stopped, too—his breathing stopped and he even stopped talking. I wanted to touch Charlemagne, his arm or his shoulder, but I was afraid. Then he said, "Ooof, that is somethin'. That is really somethin'." He looked at me, then he looked at the father. "That is something. Thank you very much for the honor of that, and I must get back to my kitchen. Thank you, thank you very much."

Back in the kitchen he put his thumb and his index finger together, very close to the point of my nose and said, "What in hell was that? Are you nuts out of your mind? Are you playing some games with me? What in the devil was that?"

I had no clue. I had cajoled him into coming out into the dining room against his will, I said, because I wanted his opinion. I was upset by the whole thing, but now I was more upset. I wanted him to explain to me what it was.

"I don't know," I said. He was so angry at me, and I was so confused I thought I might cry. I fought it though, and I didn't cry, which meant now I was angry, too. I was also afraid—I didn't know what was happening or what to say.

"What was it?" I said. "What was it with that child?"

I was used to Charlemagne's anger, how all the hatred in the world was sometimes focused through the sites of his newspapers at me, of all people, as if I were to blame, but I was as unaccustomed as him to his not knowing. His face had changed in a way that made him look old and gentle, almost—potentially—generous. I hardly recognized him.

"I think," he said, "maybe you must call the police." He stood up and went over to face the grill.

"You come with me," I said.

"No," he said. He looked at me sideways.

"I don't know what to tell them," I said.

"I don't know!" he said.

"I'm not going to call them, not by myself," I said and sat down on his bucket and crossed my arms.

"Then you forget it then," he said. "Forget it. You put up the order?"

"What order?"

He stood and wiped his big hands on the apron and stared at me.

"Do you have a wife and children back in Haiti?" I said.

He ignored the question. He was scared. Alex and Cheryl crossed between us, both of them giving us filthy looks.

"You put the order up, right now," he said.

"I don't care one little bit about the order. No order is going up until you come with me to call the police."

"What about Raymond?"

"Raymond who?"

"Raymond the manager!" he shouted.

A minute later we were out by the men's room where the phone was. I called information. I asked for the police. She said, "This an emergency?"

"No," I said. "I don't think so. I'm not sure." I whispered to Charlemagne. "Is this an emergency?" He didn't answer, as if he couldn't understand the question. His eyes focused too intensely on my nose again. Had that fly returned?

The dispatcher hesitated. "You don't think so?"

"Something strange with this baby in the restaurant here where I work," I said. "The baby looks like it might be in serious trouble."

"Please hold on," she said. "Please, do not hang up."

The phone clicked a few times and a different woman said, "Clinton County Police. This call is recorded. Is this an emergency?"

"No," I said. "I don't think so. I think maybe the emergency is already over."

"Why did you call 911?"

"I didn't call 911."

"What?"

"I didn't call 911."

"This is 911. Is this an emergency?"

"No," I said. "I don't think so."

She answered with silence.

"There is a baby in the restaurant," I said. "I don't know. She looks— wrong."

"Wrong. Wrong?"

"I don't know," I said. "She's with her mother and father. There is something really sick about it."

"The baby is sick?"

"Uh, yes. No. Maybe. Maybe worse."

"Please remain on the phone. Street address?"

"Circle Hill Diner," I said. I looked at Charlemagne. "What is the address here?" I whispered to him. He made another face.

"I don't know the street address," I said into the phone.

"Next to Donny Donuts?"

"Exactly."

I gave her my name and the phone number and we waited. Charlemagne and I hid in the dark hallway like two beaten children. I couldn't think too well and began to ramble, as I do when I'm upset. Fear had invaded Charlemagne's eyes. I wanted to soothe him, so I talked and talked.

"We must be telling Raymond," he interrupted. "You go tell Raymond the police coming."

"She told me to stay by the phone. You go tell him."

"Like this?" he said and opened his hands, indicating his dirty apron.

"So take the apron off," I said.

"Oh, no, no, no, no, no," he said.

"You were out on the floor a minute ago like that. That's what started all this."

"No, no, no," he said. "No more tonight. You want me to lose my job!"

"Okay," I said. "Take the phone. I'll go tell him."

He wagged the finger at me again. "I don't talk to no police."

"Why?" I said. "Why do I always fall for useless men?"

"Eh?"

"Charlemagne," I said. "Where did you get such a fabulous name?"

"My mother," he frowned. He turned and surveyed the dark hall and what he could see of the dining room. "She give it to me."

"You have children?" I said.

His eyes went rapidly left and right. He gave no answer, but he showed no shame. What Annie said were lies.

"Why do I always fall in love with useless men?" I repeated.

He acted like I had changed the subject. His eyes were serious when he said, "I don't know, love buggy. You in love?"

I was distracted by the phone making another clicking noise. He touched my shoulder and said again, "You in love?"

It wasn't exactly the case. The game somehow didn't fit the board, like playing checkers with a chess set. I looked at him and he looked at me and I only half-lied. "Amazingly enough," I said.

He whispered, "You got a date? You going to make some butter tonight, eh?" He made a gesture then with his knees, a kind of swooning motion that might have been taken as lewd. Fred Astaire or Frank Sinatra got away with such things, too.

"No," I said. "Probably not. Look, go tell Raymond."

"Who you in love with?"

"Forget it," I said. "Look, we have this—this thing out there in the dining room. I have the police on the phone—"

"No, no, no," he said. "You tell me." His willingness to cooperate was at its end. I began to lose nerve, to feel guilty. How many tables were out there waiting for service? Where was Raymond? Who was covering? How could I have been away so long?

"I cannot tell you," I said. "Especially you."

"Why?" he said. "Since when you don't tell me something? You always tell me too much. Now you cannot tell me an interesting thing. Why not?"

"Since it's you." I said and put the phone down on the shelf.

"Eh?"

"Since it's you," I said and tried to run but he got hold of my arm.

The girls and I sat in a booth for a long time. Raymond made two pots of coffee and kept filling our cups. He brought down a pecan pie and a gallon of vanilla ice cream and plates and forks and napkins for everybody.

Cheryl said, "He didn't even look surprised, I mean the father didn't."

"Yeah," said Annie. "But then he kind of did, like, who me? When the cops told him to stand up. Like, who are you talking to, me?"

"Yeah," said Alex. "But he was such a little mouse."

"Who was a mouse?"

"The father, if you want to call it a father."

"Can you imagine? Like, not even noticing even?"

"Jesus! I don't think I can eat."

"How long do you think it was like that, I mean, like that—"

They all looked at me. "How do I know?" I said.

"You're the one who saw," said Cheryl, her eyes distorted, accusing through her bifocals.

"What do I know?" I said. By now I was upset. "I don't work at the morgue, do I? You think I see this all the time. Maybe an hour? Two hours? A day?"

"Naw! No way."

"I never see nothing. Nothing at all," said Alex.

"I didn't even know what I was seeing," I said. "It was Charlemagne that knew."

"Where is that prick?" said Annie. She turned and surveyed the empty room. I said nothing, though I had seen him put up his apron and go out the back right after the police interviewed him. They talked to him for most of an hour. With me they spent five minutes.

"Did you see that fireman?" said Cheryl. "The one with the hat? Jesus, Mary, and Joseph! Next time my oven catches fire I'm gonna call his ass in. And tell him to bring his hose."

"What about the mother? Wouldn't you think she might have noticed?"

"What do you think?" said Annie. "Did they somehow not know? Were they pretending or something? Were they like in the grip of some bizarre kind of evil or were they like psychologically all fucked up?"

"Sometimes if something is too difficult, your mind just makes it invisible," Alex said. "Like, someone once said—I forget where I heard this—imagine how an elephant looks to a flea."

"This was two fleas. A mama and a papa flea," said Annie.

"They were cracked," said Rachel.

"That's the thing of it, isn't it? It was both of them. The two of them."

"Maybe they were on LSD. Charles Manson was on LSD."

"Didn't they put the father in handcuffs?"

"The two of them!"

"No!"

"Yes!"

"No, they did not," said Annie. She looked to me.

But I didn't know, I told them, and I told them the truth, which was that I didn't know anything. Then I almost told them how worried I was about Charlemagne, that I hoped he was all right. I wouldn't say I hoped he'd come back. I just said I didn't know. I hadn't noticed handcuffs on them. I hadn't seen.

We were quiet a minute, but I had to say something. They were all facing me a long time, then they faced me again when I said, "It was somehow as if that was me in there, in that car seat. I swear to God."

Then they all looked at me. Annie almost said something but Alex stopped her, touching her under the table. I started running on then, like I do sometimes when I've said too much and then can't stop. The thing is

I was sure all this was my fault, I said, somehow I believed just by being there at that moment I caused—somehow even arranged the whole god-forsaken thing. How else could you explain it?

The girls stared at me in horror, so I went on to tell them I was in love with Charlemagne. I told them about the call we made together and how afterwards when I told him how I felt for him, he made a strange, frightening face, like I had just cheated him out of a hundred bucks—like I had offered something he had always wanted but could never have.

"Maybe it's true," I said with emphasis, looking all around me, "the thing Annie says about him."

I told them about the phone call, when I was alone with Charlemagne in back and after he got his hand on my wrist all I could see past him was the length of the dark hallway and a crowded table in the dining room. How he put his face then, close to mine, and made a stirring motion around my nose with that big black-and-pink finger. It hurt to look, so close like that, and I found it hard to breathe, as if that finger had lodged between my ribs and my lungs; I turned my eyes away, I said, and remembered how every winter since my house burned, after things had seriously begun to freeze, when the air was so cold it made you cough, I went down Route 212 in the mornings before school to Readington Pond where Brian McGuiness died and rode my bicycle out in expanding circles onto the ice. I continued doing this even through my last year of high school. I stood up on my pedals as I went out, my feet going down and down in the slippery weightlessness until the pond began to crack and slope away under my tires.

The girls were all wide-eyed. I knew I should shut my mouth. But I also knew I had been caught in a moment that had too many implications, like the first loser who happens upon an autowreck on a back road.

Charlemagne had whispered something more, but I couldn't understand him. When they arrived, the cops used their lights but not their sirens—the blue-and-whites were flashing in the suddenly shiny, spectacular night. There had been a perfect silence, thank God, in the back by the phone, and Charlemagne holding me in the electric darkness, both his big soft hands too tight around my wrist. ✧

What We Do

Mat Johnston

Cindy, the only Korean girl I know, sees me on my front steps eating chips so she rides her bike over. Pink streamers hang off her handlebars and when her bike is dumped in my front yard, the streamers hide in grass. She comes up to me and sticks her hand in the bag of chips, makes a lot of noise, and pulls out only three. She's small and feisty, she chirps when she talks, and looks all over the place so she doesn't have to look at you. Her mom just bought her a headband and her bangs are pulled back, curling up on the middle of her head. Her hair's shiny and thin, like the rest of her. She usually chews on her lips, biting off chunks and swallowing, but she's eating chips now.

"We're practicing what we want to be," she says. She's the news spreader today, trying to get all the kids from all the houses. I see four of them on the street already. The trouble kid, Cory, is jumping up and down and screaming *ant* and then *I'm smushing the ant*. And because of him, four kids jump together using the street like a trampoline, and they all scream for a while until they're shaken and back on our earth. The fake ants are dead soldiers in the road.

"What do you want to be," I ask Cindy even though I know they're all probably just talking about it. We spend summers talking about things. Almost every girl wants to be a nurse and they use sticks for needles. Boys are lawyers. We really don't know what they do, but we have cases and we make up the rest and it usually involves things we do anyways. Lawyers throw rocks and lawyers have pistols.

"I'm a golden retriever," she says, shrugging. She doesn't ask for more chips, she just grabs them. Dogs stuff their faces in their food, Cindy just stuffs her hand in her mouth. I've pretended to be her before. I pulled back the corners of my eyes and ran into my brother's room. Then he wanted to be her and we showed our mom, who was out of focus through the slits of our eyes, telling us never to show her that again. Cindy tells me to meet everyone by the gutter later to drop rocks into it and figure out something to do. "We all have to be something," she says and pulls her bike up off the lawn. She leaves, wobbling down the driveway. My mom sticks her head out the door, a catalog is folded over, only one page showing wallpaper and what rooms look like with wallpaper. I slip under her arm, inside, where she has big plans that haven't come to anything for our own pearly walls.

My brother, Luke, has the TV on ten minutes before cartoons. He's sitting under the painting with geese and a barn, things three miles from us but kept two feet above the couch, here, as a reminder. He gets up and changes the volume, then sits down and tips his legs over the armrest. We're not in the country, but we're close enough. Sometimes there's the country hush in the air. We're bored like all the country kids we know. Except we're not dirty.

"What did she want," my mom asks. She pats a place on the couch where I'm supposed to sit. She doesn't know that everybody wants something. Cindy wants people to imagine with her. Josh wants to play trucks. Kelly wants to play house or store. Cory wants you to play in his yard so he can tell you to leave whenever he wants you to. Sam and Ryan want to play sports. I want to find things in the woods and my brother wants me to do whatever he does. He's picking his nose, from the other end of the couch. I resist.

We step outside and Luke looks down the neighborhood. House after house, everyone tries to make theirs look different, but it doesn't work. He moves out into the yard and runs to the fence, hoists himself up on it, tips his top half over the edge of it and scans the street, both ways— nothing and nothing. I see his back, but I know every part of him. He's as simple as a drawing, his face is a baby's face on a six-year-old and his hair's shaped like a bowl. You could draw him in two minutes. He's working on toughness and he tries his new whistle because he thinks it's loud; he holds the fence with one hand and crams his whistling fingers in his mouth. Nothing, he has to try three times. It's supposed to be a signal to everyone that he's here and something needs to happen. This little kid, cobalt eyes and thick brown eyelashes, the part of our father on him. He turns around and looks back at me, sets his mouth down, moves it in circles of indecision. This is a waste of time, he's thinking, someone should've already fallen off their bike or off a swing so he can run around and scream for an adult.

"Get your bike," he tells me. He wants to do a stakeout.

"I'm not getting my bike." I want to look for birds' nests even though they're dirty and my mom usually makes me wear plastic bags on my hands when I look for them. Or I could look for fossils. We've only found one cow skull in the woods. But I know Indians lived here and they're bound to show up as bones.

"You'd better get your bike," he tells me and it's a command. He's heading for his already, trying to make a gang out of the two of us.

"I'm staying here," I tell him and he walks past his bike and wheels mine over, spokes spinning.

"If you don't grab it, I'm dropping it," he says, using his eyes as force, one cheek rising.

"Don't drop it," I tell him. I just spray-painted it and I'm afraid it will chip and then it will to start to rust, and the rust will spread to the chain, and my only luxury won't move.

"Then grab it," he says, fierce pride on him. War paint and ammo for eyes.

We round up two other brothers. There's finally something to do so something big happens. I get pushed down, the breath in me shakes before it settles and sits in my stomach like a water-filled balloon. I open my eyes and that's when the sky sits down, on top of me, not heavy, just blue, and I feel a pang in my back where I hit and that goes all the way to the fingertips and then leaves. What happens next is nothing, they all think I'm paralyzed. Before this, Sam and Ryan fought about who could be the linebacker because that position is both of theirs. It's not even football season. They're wearing the jerseys they got for Christmas; Ryan's smaller because he came after Sam and their mom says they eat different anyways. Too much beef jerky is what she means. Sam's dimples are turning into big fat holes. I heard the ball bounce and tip over, into the grass. It's fresh cut and moist. Our father's mowing the lawn, but he crept in front of the house where he wouldn't be in our way. Then comes violence, like the mower that spits up branches or the sound of branches. Here's the replay: my brother came up to me and slammed his flat hands into my shoulders and that's how I'm here. His name is junk in my mouth. Luke. Like battery acid or something no one needs in their mouth to begin with.

"You don't know the rules," he says. I say the same thing back and he comes and leans over me, tries to use his sweet-looking face for something else, moving his forehead around, squinting, going into a glare, a shift of gears. *I'm angry, pussy,* he's trying to say, but it's a joke because of the rest of him—toothpaste in the corners of his mouth, white patches, mold on his lips. He's younger and does push-ups, but only when we all watch TV so we have to watch him, too. His muscles haven't grown and I'm looking back at him so hard, his muscles are going to rot.

Sam picks up the football and wedges it between his arms and his stomach fat. He's just learned to spit and he cranks his head around and spits away from us. I've seen better. Ryan checks a scab on his arm and lifts it partway, like a lid on a can. They're not our best friends, but they're our age. Their mom sends them over here without even calling our house. They're fixtures; they always want snacks.

"Stop whining," my brother tells me. He's blonde and the mean streak's stamped on his face; he's suddenly flushed with it and it's leaking its irritation on me. We go through these faces everyday. We scrape each other or pinch the elbow skin. I rubbed green grass on his new shoes and he pushed my stomach into the doorknob. We can't share a room anymore.

"Then you cooperate," I tell him. That's a new word, we cooperate in the third grade. I sit up and reach around, brush the lawn off my shirt. My brother kicks grass at me, but it doesn't go far, it just rains back down on what it's come from. Sam spits again, his eyes trail it, waiting for something to happen, a spit somersault, something acrobatic. It just splats on a tree trunk. "Come on, guys," he says and then the back door slams open and shut. Her feet on the patio, her dissatisfied sigh louder, like it's been put to a microphone. Sam squats because he doesn't know what's going to happen, that it's all useless, finally, these postures. "Let's play," he insists, hunkered down into his skin and our mother moves up right beside him. Mothers trail us, we can't sense them. She's not part of the game, but she's here as referee.

"What's going on," she asks. She's barefoot, one leg kicked out. She tells them to go home and calls us boys, shepherding us inside, saying *cookies are out of the question*, saying no to everything and then grounding us at the kitchen table for the *bologna* she saw out the window. Brothers don't hit. Luke keeps his arms crossed until he gets up and storms out, kicking his shoes off at the door. Our mom rolls her eyes at him because she knows what he's all about. I smile and ask if I can clean the bathroom. *Go into your room. I don't want to look at you either.* Then she doesn't have to. I'm in my room with a book balanced on my nose, trying to soak in everything and I can hear Luke hitting the wall or banging his head on it. If you touch the wall, you can feel it *(thud, thud)*, a heart under bones and skin. Let me out, he means, but it's good we're stuck. *Thud, thud.* The next day, all the neighbor kids are playing together and they all eat acorns and throw up. Cindy pukes on her mom's new couch. She has to hire a cleaner that comes in a van with contraptions. He's there two hours. The mothers call each other. It's the same for everyone else, puking, tucked in beds, eating Jell-O, a plastic pail next to them *in case* they retch again. Everyone's banned from eating acorns, but the things are all over the place. No one will move them. They only thing we can do now is throw them. No one knows what happens to anyone for two days. My brother and I have to sweep the porch and the house. Two days. It's like living somewhere else, no one stopping by. Clocks tick. We melt crayons on the windowsill. We go inside to air conditioning and stay there, in blankets, it's too cold, and if we leave a door open for too long, we get yelled at. *Close it.* We're told neither of us pay the bills or *if you two don't stop it* … but that sentence is never finished.

Then everyone's back. Nothing's really happened. Josh had a cavity and got put under. He lifts his top lip to show it off. Silver patches on a tooth. He thinks he can be first up to bat because of it. Stupid.

Loose kids everywhere. Some of them have gone to the gas station for baseball cards and crap to eat before lunch. Change slaps around in their pockets when they peddle. One after the other, my brother in the middle with his two quarter allowance wrapped in a hand and mine stuffed in a secret sock in a drawer. They're all boys and they won't play with girls until they get boobs, they say. But Kelly has them and we're on her front steps. "Guess what I found," she asks me. We could've gone with everyone, but we didn't. She's the biggest girl in the neighborhood, ashy hair that floats two inches above her shoulders, thick arms, thick legs. There's a hill to the store and if you're with her, you have to stop four times. We play together every day except when she has her period, which she hasn't really gotten, and she stays inside with the cramps. She actually just watches TV, where she found out about it, and doesn't answer the phone because it's not by the couch. Now, she's sticking her legs out, looking at them, big white stumps. Her shorts bunch up into her butt when we're sitting; I can tell. When we stand up to go, she'll pull at the shorts and if that's not enough, at the clogged underwear.

"Guess."

I don't know what she's found. We're sitting on her front steps, looking at what we've done to her driveway with chalk. She drew me, I drew her. Neither of them looked real and now the wind's pulling the chalk off the driveway and our pictures are getting lighter. It's June and still not warm enough, the dew stays on the grass all day or gets on your legs. We stay in the street, usually, or on the steps. Our town is two miles away and we're here, in a pocket of houses. Kelly kicks her legs out in the sun; the small hairs settle down and the goose pimples fade. Summer's not until July, that's when we really bake. "Guess, guess." Her eyes hop around, she keeps slapping at her back that's in the shade and in the mosquito territory. Our names, in big letters, face the street. So do we.

"What?" *Guess.*

I don't feel like it so I look at the ice cream pail we've filled with rocks and water. They're taking a bath and after that, we'll put them back by the dogwood bushes. All of the rocks need a bath, and we still have all day. We have to wash the chalk drawings off the driveway before her dad comes home because he doesn't like it all drawn on. The hose sits in front of us like a snake with an open mouth. We're all still. The rocks don't move in their bath.

"I found slime," she says, excited, stretching her fingers out when she lets her idea loose. Her cheeks are red, but they're always red. She huffs and puffs, even when we're sitting down. Asthma. "We should sell it," she says. There's nothing else to do and I can see her vision: everyone in the neighborhood with slime, everyone needing to buy more everyday. "I found it in the lake," she says. The lake is everyone's even though both of us live across the street from it. I'd rather not go near it, there's weeds and it's like oatmeal between your toes. I run through sprinklers. I tell her it's probably goose poop and she tells me there aren't geese in this lake. "I've got cups for lemonade," she says, excited, picking in her ear. "Let's sell it in those."

She settles everything. We take our bikes and a blanket, we dump the rocks out of the pail and scoop the goo off the lake's surface. We collect it and sell it. Cindy comes over and sits with us. Carrie, Cory's sister, rides by with three of her dolls crammed in her bike basket. She throws them in the air and lets them land on the street and rides her bike over them and then she calls the ambulance and does a siren scream, scooping them up and rushing off for surgery. Cory comes up on his bike, behind her, and stops by the curb. Kelly and him are in the same grade and I think they'll get married even if the kids would be ugly.

"What is that," he asks, sneering, saying it around a sucker that's in his mouth. Then he buys some, a nickel, and pretends to drink it before he tells us it's bad, dumping it by our feet, riding off. He stands up when he rides. He's learning pop-a-wheelies, he's not good at them, so he might tip over. He rides towards a collection of boys who've all come back from the store, plastic bags hanging off their bike handles. My brother, Alex, Josh, Sam, Ryan. And when he's there, they all go together. We're out of business.

We have to shuck the corn for dinner while our father talks to the old man with the claw hand who lives across the street. He's just a face and a name to us, bones in clothes watering his lawn. We're standing by the garbage can, tearing leaves off. Kelly and I closed our slime business and I caught frogs and put them in the old slime bucket. My brother pissed on them, so we're not talking. It took me two hours to find them and then I had to dump them out and watch them scatter. Hundreds of them. I want to ask my brother if he'd rather have a claw hand or no hand. His head's bent over the corn, pulling the sticky hair stuff out—the same color as his—and the question's burning in me, but if I talk first, he'll tell me I lost my silence and that's like stepping in shade, if it's cold, I'll wish I hadn't. He'd want a claw hand anyway, to scare people, to practice with, or to stick in the freezer and touch your skin. He's already our watered-down devil, he doesn't need a claw. He tears through the corn, ear after ear, and then our dad is loping up the driveway, waving, backhanded at the old man. His wife fishes in the morning and dumps the fish guts on her bushes. My dad takes the corn cob out of my hand and rips three leaves off at once, matching my brother.

"What'd you do today," he asks. He's close to me, the smell of him, Stetson.

I say nothing because what I want to say is he pissed on my frogs and he'd just ask what I did to make him do that.

All right. I didn't tell him Cindy and I were making brownies in her mini-oven.

*

Everyone comes out at six-thirty. Every night. Like bugs. We're waiting on the curbs.

Here comes Cory. He says his bike is a BMX, but it's not. It's still got a bell on it and he won't use it because it's sissy. There's a playing card clothespinned in the wheels. It's not even a ten-speed. It's just a bike. He goes up and down the block, the same thing over and over. You see his back or you see his face. Sometimes he'll give you the finger, but not today. My brother and I are in the neighbor's woods, picking through it to see if there's anything we want. There's golf balls, at least ten, but we leave them, we have our own. Alex's dad is yelling for their dog. It runs off, goes in other people's garages and sniffs around. It's usually tied in front of their house, by the door, like a muddy rug.

Alex's dad yells, "Brutus." He cups his hands over his mouth, standing in the yard in his work clothes. Cory streams by him, no hands on the handlebars, showoff. He yells, "Brutus," too. He yells it four times loud and passes by my brother and I without looking. Brutus, Brutus. He's louder than Alex's dad and you can hear his voice get high and scratchy, girlish. Brutus is not answering anywhere. He probably crossed the highway to the other lake or someone's hit him and there's nothing anyone can do. Cory yells and pedals. Most of the time he rides without hands, and I want him to hit a bump and fall, get a cut, cry home. Break a leg. He steers the bike back around, comes our way.

Something happened. Alex, the new kid, had to pull his pants down to get into Cory's yard. Cory is older than everyone and has stripes shaved into his head. His sister can play in their yard no matter what, her dolls get rained on because she leaves them there. Alex said that he had to go behind the air conditioning unit to do it. Three of us, my brother and him, were sitting on top of Alex's jungle gym. Our legs were through the monkey bars, looking at the lake that's smooth silk and dark green. There's a rope across it that older kids swing on, out of a tree, into the water when it's hot. Everybody's parents say that it's illegal because it's somebody's land, across there, but that person has never showed up or said anything. Cory's going to do it before school starts. If he doesn't, he owes everyone a dollar. Alex said that Cory just wants to see your underwear, it's the rules.

We asked Alex what they did in his yard. He said, kickball and I wanted to shake him until the good stuff came out. Not kickball, but Cory giggling, Cory dreaming about everyone, Cory wanting to eat all our underwear.

Kelly's up the street with Cindy. They have jump ropes and they laugh together if someone trips. Sam and Ryan are chasing a chipmunk in someone else's front yard with a butterfly net. This is the summer before they get traps. They run behind the house, darting around, never quick enough, disappearing behind a row of pine trees and Kelly and Cindy cross the street, skipping, hand in hand. You can go anywhere *(not flower gardens or in sheds or on porches)* and the only thing old people do is shoo you out or tell you to scoot. They think they know us well because they have all day to watch us, but we don't warm to any of them. We think that all their grandkids are dead and they're looking for more.

Cory's slowed down, he yells, "Flutus, Rutus, Plutus, Shutus." The whole neighborhood's got to hear him, it's always like that. He chases his sister just so she'll scream and then he'll jump on her, pin her down in the grass until someone makes him stop. He's closer, the pit-pit-pit-pit-pit of the playing card on his spokes, his brakes squeal and he puts one foot on the curb and one foot on the street. We're ten feet away and we turn to him. I'm taller than my brother and better looking. New glasses, my stomach doesn't push over the top of my shorts anymore, my mother calls my eyes burnt tangerines. But I know he's the one who already knows what to say, and if he has to, he'll throw something. I throw fits.

"What're you doing," Cory asks, putting a finger in his nose and then flicking it at us. There's nothing on it, just a gesture. He's wearing cut-off sweat pants and a shirt with a cartoon bear on it that all the elementary schools gave everyone. He has freckles, too, big, runny ones. Stains on his face. "What're you doing," I ask him back because it's just come out of me and I know the kid beside me is littler, a runty thing, and I've never acted this big before so he must be crushed with some sort of love. We know we have to stare at Cory together. I put my hands on my hips and kick a leg out. My brother wipes his mouth for no reason and wipes his hand on his shorts. Now we're staring, completely.

"I can't tell," he says and he looks around, then back to us with a sneer that's wrapped from one ear to the other. "It's top secret. If I tell you, you'll explode."

"Big deal," my brother says. He picks up a stick and cracks it apart on his knee, throwing the two pieces on the ground. He doesn't know karate. It's tough, though.

"You'll see," Cory says. "Watch." Then, it's like he's trying to think of something, hard. He stands up straight, straddling the bike, and closes his eyes. "I'm building a portal," he says after five seconds. We're not shocked, he pushes out lies like air and his eyes open back up and look at us until he's stunned, leaning back away from us. There's wind in his face, nowhere else. It's a dry monsoon.

"You exploded," he screams. "You exploded! What a mess." His foot pushes the kickstand back up, he's riding away. "Mat exploded! Brutus, Flutus! Exploded! Someone call the doctors!" He rides up to his dad, a beach ball shaped man, who's just stepped out of his Cadillac and has lit a cigarette in their driveway. Home from work. "Kapow! Explode! Mess! Mess! Ambulance! Quick!" he's screaming, dropping his bike on the grass, catching his dad's leg, and hanging off his thighs. The man hardly looks down, just brushes the top of his kid's head.

We're still here. I haven't exploded. My guts would be on my brother and right now every single part of me is beside him.

*

I hear a sharp whiz sound. Our dad found out about the frog business and told me I shouldn't collect them anyway and if I do, Luke shouldn't pee on them. Our mom said, I can't control them and this made us smile and look at each other (we're uncontrollable, us) over pork bones and bald corn cobs and the sudden realization that we've made part of her not like us. We smiled more. They're upstairs, wrapped around each other on the couch in front of *Dynasty*, nuzzling. I can't stand that, they make me sit on the floor, they kiss in commercials. The whiz sound happens again, and I don't know what it is. I get closer to the basement door and push on it, squeaking my way in and this upsets everything. He turns towards me with a BB gun, the one we're supposed to share; he cocks the handle and leans into a scope that isn't there, just a metal prong with a V in it for target practice. I'm apparently in the V.

The room gets smaller, everything, except for him, studying me, and I figure out I'm not shrinking either because he keeps the gun at the same level. I think I'm shrinking.

"Don't move."

He's being Western and so am I. My hands go up, and the sheriff's got me, I surrender. He could make me blind and then I'd have to carry around a stick or get an ugly retriever. He doesn't know the rest of his lines, so we're just standing there. I hear the room and the dryer, rivets on jeans scraping the drum. He'd go to foster care and write us Christmas letters. And then the real thing in front of me, the brother, starts saying two things at once, but his lips aren't moving. I'm making him talk in my head. *This has been a long time coming. I'm going to blow your brains out.* I can see him think, falling back into every instance of his real self. He asks me, *who do you think you are* and the non-speaking part of him holds steady even when the house starts humming and some water is running in pipes. The blonde person is smiling and squinting, one eye closed, looking at me. I'm pickling in the cold of the basement and in my icy skin. He snorts because the idea's finally come to him. This can't be shown up.

"You have to help me tomorrow or I'll shoot you."

I'm not shot. I'm in the tree with him the next day.

Our parents pull two chairs to the edge of the patio and sit. We're fifteen feet above them, in an oak; if either of us fell out, it'd be the end. We'd be in the paper and we'd get cookies from everyone and bars, brownies, things made from cereals. Our mom winces when she sees us go from branch to branch while our dad judges the lawn. She relaxes when we've made it up, but even then, she shouts things at us. Usually one word: *boys*, her usual. I look at them, whispering, cupping their words in hands. It doesn't matter. We're too high up. We see roofs, not them anymore.

"We need a wall first," my brother says. He's wanted help all summer for his fort and now, I'm here. It's just a flat place, not like everyone else's forts that came from stores. I tell him I see Miss Politiski in her swimsuit and he comes over to the edge of the fort and grabs the branch above him, lifts his legs, and swings a little. We both look over into the next lawn. She walks in between her laundry that's hanging and then it's just her thigh behind pants and shirts, extra skin like a frown above her knees. "She looks naked," I tell him and she pulls a pair of pants off the line and is re-clothed. She throws them on her shoulder, her mouth holding all the clothespins, and moves further down the line. When she sunbathes, she does it with a towel over her precious face.

"She's ugly," he says, but it's just words. He's thinking of the wrong person, the lady across the street and three doors down who's just a beast. Too old and looking too young. Our mother says that if we ever catch her like that, lock her up. This woman's an old guy's second wife, they water-ski and drive around in his Cadillac. Her makeup's a pound and she has no women friends. Miss Politiski goes inside and our view is bare. Leaves.

"Look there," I tell my brother. I point to the road. Alex's crossing the street with Cindy, they hit Cory's front yard. It's mostly weeds because his dad won't spray the lawn. You can't go barefoot there or even have a Slip-n-Slide because it'll tear. Cory runs to them, out of his garage, throwing a ball up and screaming until he's caught it, hugging it tight to his chest. We focus, we make our hands binoculars and they go around the side of the house. Then we don't know what happens. We watch to make sure it's taking them ages and after twenty seconds, it really must be happening *(by the shrub or the air conditioner, shorts around ankles, backside, frontside)*. I turn to my brother and put my hands on the top of my shorts. He has no idea what this is about or what I'm going to do. I squat and pull my shorts part way down and wag my butt at him. We have the same underwear; our mom buys packs of ten and splits them up and, now, he has to show his to me, too — the same thing but he pulls his farther down so his butt-crack is showing, a crease of skin. A peach.

He says, "Oh, Cory. My pooper."

I say, "My undies are pretty. Let's play ball."

"Smell it," my brother says. I start laughing and he shrieks the words out. "It's greasy," he's saying and wagging it, pulling them down, inch by inch, so it's just plain skin, like a face without anything on it. His shorts go to his knees and his underwear follow them down part way and then get caught around his thighs. You can see all of them, a brown patch riding down the middle like a road in a picture. Mine are back up, I'm sealed in; his butt's white, oh man.

"Full moon," he screams.

I shut my eyes and howl for real, a werewolf, a pretty bad howl, but it makes his legs shimmy and his little butt's dancing and bouncing fifteen feet up. We're hidden in leaves, we're being animals; we do projects on animals in school, our mother will say we're learning and our father will smile because he knows how to call pigs. I get an itch. I lean forward and smack him so hard it stings my hand and his skin turns pink and prickles. He stands up straight and wiggles back into everything and turns to me. I have a devil grin that slinks into an apology. I get warm, in my feet first, and it crawls up by my ears. He blows some air into one of his cheeks and breathes in through his nose, trying to decide what part of him to let out. I think I'm red.

Highways make cars go by and then a semi.

I hear someone's phone ringing and then it's ours because I hear the scrape of a chair on the patio and farther out, from the side of the house *(the shrub, the air conditioner, the looking)*, Cory screams mercy in his back yard, looking like every kid in the afternoon's last hour. The three of them are squeezing each other's hands, in a circle, pushing into each other, their faces squinched. Mercy. We know that game.

"That hurt," my brother says, incredulously, and he's forming a smile, a half-one. I'm not red anymore, that fades, and then I'm lightweight. We don't know what to do now, he reaches around and touches where I smacked him. There's a grimace, an astonished cheek rising to an eye. We're wild to no one because nobody could see us and we couldn't see them. Nothing's ever happened anywhere.

The sun's pushing itself in all the windows, rectangles of light on the floor, and we're at the kitchen table. I'm eating all of the marshmallows out of my cereal before the real day can begin. Luke pours himself another bowl, half of it goes on the counter. "Ninety-five degrees today, boys," our mother says, running around the house in her swimsuit. We can smell her trail of hairspray. "What do you two think you're doing taking your time," she asks. I just shrug and attempt a smile, a little milk falls out of my mouth and runs down my chin. "Get ready," she says. "We're tanning. Pronto. Your suits are on your beds." She puts on her sun block, she puts the stereo on the window's ledge, she runs outside like it's a cause for joy and not heat stroke and yells at us to move our little legs. Luke stands up and stomps to his room; I look out the window and see the whole yard filled with brassy light and it seems like an occasion, like we've rented it all. Our mother sits down in her sun chair, adjusts the back, and lies down, unhooking the straps to her bikini. No lines. My swimsuit's on my bed and I drop my underwear to the floor and slip it on. Luke comes to my room in his undersized shorts, two years too old for them, his thighs giving way to chicken legs and his ankles, his scrawniest edition. We're brothers since I spanked him. We look at each other different. I see a little kid who's put on his dumb sunglasses and is thinking about T-ball while I'm thinking about him, all boyish. The butt I spanked probably smells.

"Are you ready," he asks, sullen as he can get, reaching around to itch himself on the shoulder. I tell him I am and he leads the way, through the house, outside. Then the world restarts. There's a bang, an explosion, something happening. *In the air or on the ground somewhere or here* and we stop like animals who want to sniff the air. Our mother sits up, disturbed from wherever she was and looks around but there's no sound anymore and Luke and I just stand at the edge of the patio and wait for her to tell us what it was. No dust settles, just the noise that clears so we can hear the radio again, the Farmer's report, on every hour.

I say, "Mom. Accident," because of the highway and because I'm sensible. A pileup. A collision. Or some dog, finally flattened, having flirted with the road for too long. We walk towards her, sitting up straight, a stalk of corn in our own back yard, and she tells us to lay down while she runs inside to make some calls. She has two towels for us, she wants us to crumple in the sun, to drink pops with her, to be her boys today, and there's something durable about us, our stomachs going into the hard earth while she can stay all day in our only lawn chair, and we're supposed to flip around, back and forth, like pancakes. We've forgotten about explosions. Luke says he hates tanning, I tell him I hate him, he tells me, no I don't, and our mom comes running back outside, five minutes later, bare feet, hopping on one leg once she's stepped on a stick. She has the news because a hand's on her mouth and she's not worried about sucking her stomach in. She's let it hang out, a medium-sized pouch. It's the very beginning of everyone covering their mouths. Wide eyes. It's exactly what Cindy tells me the next day when she has me over for lemonade. I'm not supposed to tell anyone, but I leak it everywhere. And we're secretly proud we knew first, stirring our sugar water on her front steps and watching the neighborhood do nothing. Just the old people now, the people who don't know Cory and Josh were playing in Josh's dad's semi and they hit the shift stick and put it out of park and it rolled across the street and crashed into Kelly's house. The noise, *bang, wham, crash*, whatever it was. Cindy lets her eyes go crazy, stiffens herself, has to talk to my ear. Old people can't imagine Cory and Josh with their pants down. Or what happened yesterday, Cory playing doctor with Kelly and shoving his sister's twirling baton up her in his fort. Now, she's home with her mom. It's like the acorn business all over again. Cindy asks if anything happened to me and then she's quiet, thinking, and I can't know everything even if I want to know what happened to the twirling baton, if Cory's sister even knows, if she's outside now, playing with it in her own empire of grass. Up in the air, into the hand, majorette.

Now our mother always, forever wants to know if anything's wrong. Our smallest whimpers need Band-aids. We're only allowed in our yard.

*

I see Cindy walking in the street, wolfish, kicking whatever she finds into the gutters. I wave her over. We've been forced into being best friends because of all the information. When she sees me, she runs, grabs my hand and I lead her in the back yard, where the slow action of the afternoon is happening. Sam and Ryan are in the tree fort with my brother. They have two hammers and other things taken from our garage that need to be nailed up. A long piece of chicken wire stretches between two branches now and it was supposed to be a wall that no one could see through, but we changed our minds. Now it's for the birds so they can't get in; we've decided it's going to work and we'll wake up one morning and there will be a whole flock of them stuck in it, their heads poking through the wire and their wings flapping and grappling around in the air they're hanging in. Cindy and I look up at them. Cindy stomps her foot down on mine, something she's never done before, and asks me what we're doing. I don't know what we're doing, we're standing here, marooned in the yard. "Listen," she says and it's forceful. She's been like this lately, she had her birthday and got everything she wanted and she hasn't had time to be bored. No one has. Kelly's been inside her house for a week and Josh, too, but he doesn't come out as much anyways. And Alex was inspected by Cory three times. We don't know how or what happened or where but we've guessed and my brother and I have decided that Cory took a water pistol and sprayed it up Alex's butt. Then we wonder about everyone else and how we can tell if anything happened to them. Cindy's meaner now so maybe Cory put a Hot Wheel in her, and Sam's been swearing so he could've had his penis measured. And we've decided that Cory made his sister eat her poop for a year.

"I want you to come with me," Cindy says and she starts tossing and whipping her hair around, for no reason. I tell her I can't and it's true, we need permission and I think I want to go in the tree anyway. The boys float in air. She uses her bottom lip, *please, please.*

"Where are you going?" I ask her.

She doesn't know and she gives that away by looking flustered and the boys in the tree scream bombs away all at once and drop down a piece of wood that they don't need. It lands in the brush and wasn't as exciting as they thought it would be, but they stand up there for five seconds looking glorious, looking down, the fronts of their shoes over the edge like tongues. *That was neat.* Cindy throws her hand at them, meaning they're dumb, and then she looks back at me to see if I've figured that out, too. We're all dumb. She just wants to build an office or make me be a dog so she can be the owner and the boys in the tree just want to stay up there all day and throw things at squirrels and burp and rate burps. The neighborhood makes its noise around all of us, lawn mowers, snickering in trees, the faucet inside, a girl running up the driveway, a car horn, Kelly crying in her house, Alex crying in his house, Josh crying in his house and their mothers making chicken soup.

Cindy grabs my hand and pulls me; she's insistent, and both of her hands squeeze into mine, her legs lock into the ground, and she says, "Hurry," even though there isn't one. There's nothing happening today and nothing's happening tomorrow. We've had a whole string of time, a month, one giant Sunday after another, no weeks and no days and taking our bikes out and seeing each other and pretending that things need to get done because dinner is soon or swim lessons or the porch lights are going to come on and that means one thing, come home. She's yanking now, with her eyes closed. I know that she doesn't have any plans, that she'll make it up on the spot, once she's got me going, and I don't want to see what any of it is. A cloud hides the sun, the boys throw another piece of wood, our mom answers the phone, our dad pulls up in the garage and goes inside. She lets go. Stumbles back and acts like she's going to fall. If Cory did anything to her, you can't tell. It's not a cut.

She screams, "You're boring me," and the boys scream, "Look. Look. Look."

Up there, they've found another edge to stand on, fixed there, looking, until whatever it is has gotten better and my brother, on the outside of the other two, the boss of us all, uses his whistle, a bad whistle, mostly air, to get us to look, too, but he doesn't mean from down here, he means from up there. He's scooping air with his hand, pulling it towards him even though he doesn't want the air, he wants us. Up there with all of them. And the motion becomes more frantic, faster, until it's just a hand fanning a face, signaling what he meant earlier and still signaling it when I'm up the new ladder with Cindy behind me and all three of them whispering a word, quick, that sounds like still air. The landing groans under us, five people now, and we look out where they were pointing, but their hands are falling because the moment has turned into another. It's gone. *Him*, they say, his new name. *Bringing out the trash.* Just houses now or smoking grills or antennas like bones sticking straight up on top of the houses or someone coming out but not him who we want like an actor or an encore or something better than my brother calling me Kelly as a joke and me turning to him in the bathroom with my toothbrush in my mouth last night and trying hard to say *Oh, Cory* through all the foam to see what he would do to me. ✧

Untitled as of Yet

Sarah Nankin

My mother says don't let the cigarette hang out your mouth it looks cheap. She says lots of things look cheap: cigarette burns, tight blue sweaters, coming home in the same outfit you left in the night before.
   She can never wait to be herself. She's always bleaching her lion's mane and giving me her empty bottles. Underneath the flickering bathroom light, with a halo of smoke and gnats around her head, a bare naked bulb is crusted in dust making us look gray. Nobody wants to look at themselves in a gray dusty lightbulb. My mother calls bright lights divorce lights. If yer husband saw what you looked like in em he'd divorce ya.
   I think Tiny's a queer she says. He just don't look right his head always falling back and forth. What woman would want him no money no teeth no brain plus he's filthy and how long he gonna live all up in that little room with Rocky? Those men have rocks in their heads. I tell her there is a difference between rocks and being drunk all the time. How can they be queers ma when they can't even get it up? Shut up she says what do you know about it.
   I know things in my head. Tiny always comes to fix things and drink my mom's beer. His eyes are all over and she laughs from a low place that echoes ugly in my ribs. I know that when she leans down real low with her cigarette dangling and her bad beer breath swirling Tiny's eyes are climbing the wrong wall. Her eyes spit daggers at me while her mouth gets real tight and she tells him I got nothing to climb, but I know his eyes are diggin' in sharp like the dog's teeth.
   Her roots are disappearing and I bet she feels like a whole new person now. A whole new person in the same tight blue stretchy pants and t-shirt that has a pink bear saying I love Virginia Beary Beary Much on it. The bear has a rip across one of its googley eyes and it looks retarded. If she had a husband he'd divorce her. Anyways she's not so new cause we are still sitting here in the bathroom, not somewhere else.
   More bleach and then more. I'm sitting on the toilet kicking the base one tap two tap three tap will you please just shut the fuck up with that tapping please I am trying to concentrate. I hold the empty toilet paper tube up to my eye. She looks a lot smaller through one eye. Her voice is still big.
   Come here make sure I got it all. She lowers her head and makes me check for blank spots. The smell of bleach burns my nose and I know I am going to cough right on her head. Goddamn you go outside I can do this myself.

Who taught you to cough on someone's head anyways? Go to Tiny's and play with the dogs or something. I think of Tiny's doughy hand poking me in the chest over and over and his whiny ugly wheezy laughing. I think maybe sometimes Tiny isn't queer so I get my bike instead. I ride around in circles stiffening up my muscles. My back is straight and my chest is stickin out. There's nothing there, but my mother says do it anyways. I will be prepared. Be prepared for what? When she looks at me with her mouth shut tight I think I know. ✧

Activist

Andrew Richmond

Everything in the kitchen smells fried—thirteen suitcases, eight clocks, sixteen folding chairs, two each of most appliances, six televisions, three typewriters, and twelve umbrellas. I plug in a deep fryer and drop two frozen chicken legs into the grease.

The Dachshund Bert runs in with his long claws tapping against the linoleum, wagging his tail for me to fork the chicken from the fryer and put the legs on the floor. The refrigerator shutters on two pieces of wood like skis and its motor dangling from the underbelly.

I pour salt and water into a coffee cup. A townie is through the window, in the yard, dancing a jig in polka dot boxers, black socks, and clogs. He's usually jerking through town, whistling at passing cars. It's said he'd been in an accident and can't feel temperature. He stops and gives me a straight face stare. I gargle and then spit into the sink.

The Dachshund Bert waits for his chicken. "I know, I know . . . I hate Kansas, too," I say.

The townie speaks something I can't make it out; says it again.

"What?" I still can't understand him and open the window.

". . . Activist."

"You're going to freeze to death one day townie."

"My mom's in heaven. Know how I know?"

"No," I say.

"She lives through me as her vessel," he says.

I want to say something about opting for a different model.

"Her mom took her to Florida so she didn't have to go to school no more. And she go to run around on the beach and got sand in her veins," he says.

"How'd she get sand in her veins?"

"She's in heaven. Know how I know?"

I want to say something about the weight of wet sand—how she'd be so heavy, too heavy to be an angel. "Yeah."

"Activist," he says.

"For what?"

The townie laps his bottom lip up over his top lip then says, "Bumper stickers."

The legs are small and burnt, crumbling apart when I try to pull them out of the grease. The Dachshund Bert noses over the linoleum thinking he's missed something. The more you talk to crazy people the more act like them. My mother said that once. "We are all volunteers." I say that dropping two more legs into the fryer.

I unlock the door to the stairway and begin to climb over the stacks of newspaper, a shoehorn. There are ghosts hiding behind doors, under beds, tucked in memory boxes and picture trunks. They hide inside the rolled up flags propped in a corner from when my father ran the voting poll. The last year that happened my mother left us in her sleep.

What I'm looking for is the picture of the old fashioned floozies playing poker with their derringers tucked in their garter belts and whiskey on the table. Really it's my mother and her sisters on vacation in Branson. They were a healthy bloodline.

The boards work against each other in a different room. It's a woman wearing a low-hemmed dress, wet and salt smelling. Her hems are frayed, and she is spilling through her seams. We lay on the floor with my head on her breast. She has been cast to Earth forever. I might take her in, offer remedies though I will never share a grave with her.

Police cars chase other cars in the television. I'm in the recliner laughing at the people who are crashing and spinning. I'm laughing at the people who are laughing. The Dachshund Bert peeks over the armrest of the recliner.

"Hasta mañana, John Boy," I say. "Go to bed."

He stays.

"I don't think you understand how funny that is," I say. "You know, every episode ends with that sequence with the windows of the house and each light turning off. They say goodnight ma and goodnight pa until there's one light left and then it turns off and someone says goodnight John Boy. Why that's so funny is because I was wondering if that show was ever syndicated in Spanish, if they'd say, hasta mañana, Juan Chico."

The Dachshund Bert heads back into the kitchen to lick the linoleum.

"It just wouldn't work in Spanish," I say. "They're nearly fucking Quakers."

A man comes on stage and imitates a golf swing. The audience cheers. When I'm asleep I'm in this house—unrolling ghosts, pinning flags on the wall but upside down. ✧

THEATRE POST ROAD

Jonathan Ames

Photo: Dona Ann McAdams

This photo is from my appearance in Eric Bogosian's play, *Notes From Underground*, and the only connection to the Dostoevsky work of the same title is the same title, though there are some thematic parallels. Mr. Bogosian, in addition to writing the piece, also directed me. In it I play a madman reading from his diary. At the time of this writing of this note to you, I am in the third week of a four-week run at Performance Space 122 in New York City. One interesting aspect of this production is that audience members keep having seizures or fits of some sort. One man fell right onto the stage, but because of the lights—they are blinding; I can't see a thing; I *hear* the audience—I couldn't tell what was going on. I thought someone was disgusted with my performance and had left in a huff, knocking his chair to the stage. I didn't know it was actually a body that made that odd noise just ten feet in front of me. The man was revived with a glass of water, and when the disruption seemed to be over—when there was silence—I continued with my performance.

About these texts:

For my own performances as a monologuist/storyteller, I do not memorize scripts. I simply write out a sheet (by hand) of what I call "headlines"—the main points of the story. I write up this sheet the day of the performance and then look over it several times. All the stories I tell on stage are stories from my life, so I don't feel the need to memorize them; I know them, and I write up the sheet so that I don't forget an important point or a funny one-liner. Below are typed-up versions of two of my sheets/stories: "Deep in Queens" and "The Story of My Son" (with the original for comparison). I'm not sure when the performance of "Deep in Queens" was; this sheet was loose. I keep all my "sheets" in an old suitcase and it's a disorganized mess. And this sheet was clearly a part of a night when I told more than one story, because usually I notate on the first sheet the location (theater, nightclub, etc.) and date of the show, though I estimate it to be 1997 or 1998. Both "Deep in Queens" and "The Story of My Son" were incorporated into my one-man show of storytelling, *Oedipussy*, which I performed at Performance Space 122 in 1999, and which I also presented at a few European venues and some nice American colleges.

Deep in Queens

* Porky Pig falling through the air changing into a girl as he fell
* Desire to be a girl for ten minutes when I was four or five after seeing cartoon
* Told a friend. Demeaned me. Then I forgot about it, stored it in my lower back & came out right after I started puberty.
* Read Krafft-Ebing
* Read about men who wore women's clothing
* Mujeradoes/Indians/took bravest warriors and feminized them, weakened their testicles through excessive horseback riding
* I tried to simulate this by cantering on my ten-speed
* Dressed in mother's clothes one time—despair
* Gave it up for years, then in my twenties I was writing this failed novel called "The Jewish Duke of Windsor"
* Novel about testicle, cross-dressing, anglophilia
* Friend tells me about this bar in NY called Edelweiss
* Drove in from NJ to do research
* Meet Wendy, gorgeous transsexual, Sophia Loren look-alike
* Beautiful breasts—Oedipal
* Go to L. Eastside then Queens, my great aunt lives in Queens
* Go to Wendy's place * I hold her
* Clothes on, she's naked *
 I feel her breasts, spoon her
* She says: Do you want to be my husband?
 I ejaculate
* A single phrase from her soul and I come
* Have to leave
* Out to my car
* Driving along under the elevated train, lost 'deep in Queens'
* A lion leaps at my car
* A lion that must have escaped from the zoo * Ham it up
* Realization of what it was
* Bring out stuffed lion that was dropped at my car from the elevated subway
* Recreate Porky Pig falling again
* Later, called my friend, I said: I had a strange sexual experience. Were there animals, he asked. Yes, I said. What kind? he asked. A lion, I said. That's dangerous, he said.
* End

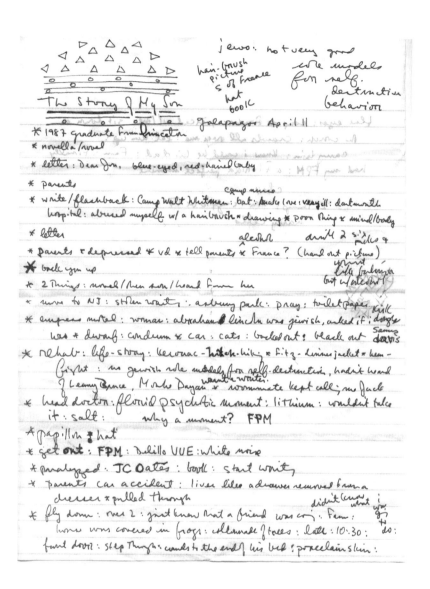

jews: not very good
hair-brush   role models
picture   for self-
s of France   destruction
hat   behavior
book

The Story of My Son   galapagos April 11

* 1987 graduate from Princeton
* novella/novel
* letter: Dear Jon. blue-eyed, red-haired baby
* parents
                    Camp nurse
* write/flashback: Camp Walt Whitman: bat: knfele love: very ill: dart month
    hospital: abused myself w/ a hairbrush * drawing * poor thing * mind/body
* letter
                        alcohol   drink 2 six packs &
* parents & depressed * vd * tell parents * France? (hand out picture)
* back you up   your
                                          like ferloryin
* 2 things: novel/then son/heard from her   but w/ alcohol
* move to NJ: stolen wait: asbury park: pray: toilet paper
                                                            kirk
* empress motel: woman: abraham lincln was jewish, asked if: doogle
    was * dwarf: condnum * car: cats: backed out! black out   same
                                                                 davis
* rehab: life-story: kerouac - hitch-hike * Fitz - livives jacket * hem-
    ingway: no jewish role models for self-destruction, hadn't heard
    of Lenny Bruce, Moshe Dayan * roommate kept call; me Jack
                        wantt a writer:
* head doctor: florid psychotic moment: lithium: wouldn't take
    it: salt: why a moment? FPM
* papillon * hat
* get out: FPM: Delillo VUE: white noise
* paralyzed. JC Oates: book: start writing
* parents car accident: liver like a drawer removed from a
    dresser * pulled through
                                              didn't know   i
* fly down: row 2: just knew that a friend was coming: fam: what up
    house was covered in frogs: collonade of faces: late: 10:30: to: do:
    front door: step through: comes to the end of his bed! porcelain skin:

The Story of My Son

Galapagos April 11

* 1987 graduate from Princeton
* novella/novel
* parents
* write/flashback: Camp Walt Whitman: bat: make love: very ill: dartmouth hospital: abused myself w/ a hairbrush * drawing * poor thing * mind/body
* letter
* parents * depressed * vd * tell parents * alcohol * france?   drink 2 six packs and vomit, like bulimia but with alcohol
* back you up
* 2 things: novel/then son/heard from her
* empress motel: woman: abraham lincoln was jewish, asked if i was: kirk douglas, sammy davis * dward * condrum * car: cats: backed out: black out
* rehab: life-story: kerouac — hitch-hikin * fitz — dinner-jacket * hemingway — fight * no jewish roles for self-destruction, hadn't heard of Lenny Bruce, Moshe Dayan wasn't a writer * roommate kept calling me Jack
* head doctor: florid psychotic moment: lithium: wouldn't take it: salt why a moment? FPM
* papillon: hat
* get out: FPM: Delillo VUE: white noise
* paralyzed: JC Oates: book: start writing
*parents car accident: liver like a drawer removed from a dresser * pulled through
* fly down: over 2 : just knew that a friend was coming, didn't know what i was going to do: farm : house was covered in frogs : colonnade of trees: later: 10:30: front door: step through: crawls to the end of his bed: porcelain skin: blue eyes: coup de foudre: pierced w/ love: sit down on couch: crawls all over me: eat him up: had my FPM: a Florida perfect moment
clap
2 things: son is going to be 17
hairy calls ✧

blue eyes: coup de foudre: pierced w/ love: sit down on the couch: crawls all over me: eat him up. carry him: Knew i could be his dad: Fam: Finally had my FPM: a florida perfect moment

clap

2 mugs: smile ...to be 17
hairy calls

RECOMMENDATIONS

POST ROAD

MIDDLEMARCH by George Eliot

Donna Morrissey

If there's anyone out there who hasn't read *Middlemarch*, please, start marching—straight to your nearest second hand store and swipe it off the shelf—yup, for two bucks, it'll be the greatest steal of your life, especially if you're a writer. When I started my first novel, *Kit's Law*, I was lost as to how far to go into the tears, the anguish, the shuddering depths where emotion takes us. And always my critics (those in my head, and those anxiously reading my drafts) were advising, 'Careful, careful, don't overwrite, don't overwrite, you're overwriting, Donna, pull back.'

But darned if I would listen. My mentor was (and will always be) Miss George Eliot, the greatest literary mind of the nineteen century, with lines like:

> ... he was a cock who thought the sun had risen to hear him crow ... ,

or

> Perhaps the wind wails so in winter for the summers dead, and all sad sounds are nature's funeral cries for what has been and is

Check this out:

> There was something horrible to Dorothea in the sensation which his unresponsive hardness inflicted on her ... it is in these acts called trivialities that the seeds of joy are for ever wasted, until men and women look round with haggard faces at the devastation their own waste has made, and say, the earth bares no harvest of sweetness—calling their denial knowledge.

More than just profundities, *Middlemarch* is the most inclusive piece of literature I've yet to read, dealing on a grand scale with locality, politicks, profession, religion, yet taking no ground from the richness of her characters—and what a crew: Dorothea, an almost modern day woman searching for a meaning in relationship and work amongst the stifling nineteenth-century morals; Casaubon, the snide, older man she marries whose lofty professional work turns into a whale and swallows him whole; Lydgate, a virile, hard-working doctor who falls in love with the darling doll, Rosamond Vincy and tries to create an angel out of the selfish, spoiled vixen; Will Ladislaw, an outspoken young man with a twisted past connecting him to Casaubon, and a passion for Casaubon's wife, the saintly Dorothea; and there's the mixed-up Fred, Rosamond's gambling brother, and Mary, poor and plain, but desired by Fred, and Raffles, an evil vagabond with an evil past, and his worthwhile victims whose immoral past catches up with their moral present, wrecking their affluence in a community they once reigned with a moral hand.

Can there be more?? Oh yes, the story itself. From start to finish we are immediate voyeurs, a fixture within Elliot's three dimensional writing, the intrigue, drama. Whenever I falter, fumble or despair with a piece of writing, I pick up *Middlemarch*, let the pages fall open, and read for a moment, and never ever have I not gone back to my story, inspired, eager and bubbling. Elliot is a genus, and *Middlemarch* a profundity of all time.

And boy, when I walk past those little, bitty publishing houses who rejected my newly written book because t'was 'Overwrote, overwrote,' I clutch my national bestsellers to my breasts and crow like the cock who knows that on this day, surely, the sun has risen just for her . . . ✧

RECOMMENDATION
THE SAVAGE GIRL by Alex Shakar

Henry Presente

The Savage Girl is a savage beast of a book. It's hard not to be torn to the ground by Alex Shakar's raging animal of a novel. It is the thematic sequel to his first widely published foray into fiction, *City In Love*, a gentle collection of short stories that updated two-thousand-year-old fables into modern terms. That dulcet creature highlighted how people have gradually redirected the divinity of nature into a spirituality of urban dwelling. *The Savage Girl* begins its romp from that fertile conclusion— Shakar presents the spirituality of the city as a given, and focuses in from that vantage.

The book's forceful forward stride is powered by its story, the legs of the novel. Ursula Van Urden is a failed painter, just moved to Middle City —New York transposed to the top of a volcano—to help care for her younger sister, Ivy. Though Ivy's nervous breakdown has temporarily halted her blossoming career as a model, it proves to be a professional catapult for Ursula. When Ursula goes to visit Ivy's ex-boyfriend, Chas Lacouture, determined to wrestle an understanding from him as to why Ivy would slice herself with a razor blade and run crazed through the streets of Middle City, she also snares a new job.

Chas's company, Tomorrow Ltd., comprises a small group of trendspotters. This eclectic group of four combs the city searching for the latest developments in style to predict the next hot thing for Tomorrow's brand-name clientele. Their means are as convoluted as their industry, and Ursula's training and apprentice eyes splendidly reveal their bizarre methodology.

One trendspotter prefers to work from home, sweating on the latest exercise equipment and soaking in virtual style as six televisions wired with a global satellite feed automatically switch to random channels at regular intervals. Another spends a month in the supermarket following children begging their fathers for cereal and watching overweight women buy boxes of laundry detergent labeled "NOW FAT FREE." One frequents posh restaurants and orders "everything popular this week." While waiting for the meal, he notices that the businesspeople a table away are using the words "good" and "bad" as opposed to the once-fashionable "sensible" and "inadvisable," and concludes that people are longing for a simpler, moral universe. The trendspotters' methods strain to learn which underlying desires are powering consumer choices that year . . . and more importantly, which will be most persuasive next year.

These underlying desires, Shakar argues, evolve purposefully like an organism. It's in this evolution that *The Savage Girl* lets you know that it's more than a beast with a good story to help you devour pages. *The Savage Girl* doesn't just ponder the present fashions humanity is feasting upon; it thinks about our next meal. As Ursula's career skyrockets and she drives a new savage aesthetic into the marketplace at the expense of family and friends, she struggles to reconcile two possible futures that Shakar aims at her. Her mental conflict shines through *The Savage Girl's* eyes with mischievous sparkle.

Early on in her training, Chas tells Ursula that:

surfaces [are] all people have . . . Look around you. How many of these people do you think ever get to experience a great passion, a great love, a great cause? A product can stand in for those experiences. A surface can stand in for the depths most people will never know.

While the assertion embitters Chas, it nurtures Javier Delreal, a fellow trendspotter who moons over Ursula. Javier is wounded by the same ugly city Ursula is struggling to come to grips with, but sees the beauty displayed in car commercials and common superstitions as effective medicine for the urban ailment.

Chas and Javier both believe that the world is coming to the end of an era—the era where irony sells products. But they have diametrical views as to what the postironic age will entail. Shakar lifts his angel, Javier, to the "Light Age," the age where people will be able to use consumerism to create their own ideal "realities." Where street punks' fashion sense, an object of public ridicule and punk solidarity, will enable them to grow into people unafraid of political derision and able to organize and rally around a common cause.

Then Shakar presents his devil, Chas, and his "Lite Age," in which the "realities" Javier asserts will set people free, will in fact just be better hidden illusions coating a far grimmer, subterranean reality. Chas believes that he can make people eat shit, if only Nestle would use the right marketing plan. If I can make people eat shit, Chas says, "then my work here will be done."

As Ursula climbs toward material success, Shakar embeds within her a volatile internal discord as she tries to decide whether "Light" or "Lite" is right and inevitable.

But *The Savage Girl* is more than a compelling story with thoughtful underwiring. Shakar's book is a beast that makes its points with claws that grip—the gimmicks are fantastic. One of Ursula's first lessons is in paradessence, Shakar's term coined to describe the promised impossibilities of a product that make it attractive to a consumer. Coffee? Waking up in the morning and comforting warmth. Stimulation and relaxation.

Ice cream? Licking and sucking against a backdrop of ice cream trucks in small towns in summertime. Eroticism and innocence.

Shakar intersperses enough tricks and humor to allow the book to theorize without preaching.

The Savage Girl is a complete animal. Its fleshy story hangs compellingly from its ideological backbone. Its characters demand empathy. And even if Shakar's racing beast of a novel slows down towards the crawl of a not entirely satisfying ending, we can't help but forgive the panting beast. After all, *The Savage Girl* runs so fast for so long. ✧

RECOMMENDATION
ITALIAN DAYS by Barbara Grizzuti Harrison

Karl Iagnemma

To call Barbara Grizzuti Harrison's *Italian Days* a travel book is to diminish it, by lumping it with so many went-there-saw-that narratives that feel like little more than dandified Fodor's guides. True, *Italian Days* describes a journey, but its odd, charming structure makes it impossible to classify: this is travel literature as memoir, mixed with art history, leavened with meditations on art and food and family and culture—often within a single page. If that sounds hectic, it is, but *Italian Days* possesses a rare voice, so captivating that readers would follow it anywhere. The effect is like reading a best friend's travel journal—a genius best friend, a friend blessed with insight and compassion and gorgeous prose.

Italian Days is organized around Ms. Harrison's trip through Italy in the mid-1980s, each chapter titled for a region she visits as she winds her way from Milan to Calabria. As a guide, Harrison's tone is usually optimistic; occasionally she is nostalgic or melancholy or irritated or sour, and her mood informs her perceptions to give her observations an unvarnished feel:

> My dinner of scotch and chocolate and fruit may have ill disposed me; on the day I visited the Pinacotera Brera, no painting—neither brooding Madonna nor pale Crucifixion—would come alive for me.

Her prose unwinds in an engaging, lumpy stream: some sections are sentence-length fragments (a transcription of graffiti in the elevator in the Uffizi; a rumor of car thieves operating out of the Roman catacombs); some are accounts of conversations (a discussion with an embittered American priest in Rome is particularly memorable); some are menus of elaborate dinners and simple lunches (Ms. Harrison writes about food with a gusto that provokes hunger). The book feels, at times, like a sidestreet in Naples: crowded and jostling, a feast for the senses, thrillingly alive.

It's probably impossible to evoke the feel of this book by quoting passages, but here goes. In St. Peter's, the author's impressions of the Pietá:

> In front of the Pietá (violent, personal, mystical): "It must be very hard to lose your son at that age," a woman says. "But he was God!" her male companion says, with more assurance than I have that His being God made it easier for Mary, who must have taken pleasure in His first step and first tooth and first word and all the ordinary things—even after, at the age of twelve, He went into the Temple (confusing and disarming her) to do His Father's business.

"The most important thing," another man says, "the most important thing is the muscles ..."

This is vintage Harrison: the conflation of the spiritual and the personal, the beautiful and the mundane. Like any good travel writer, Harrison is a keen observer, but what makes *Italian Days* feel transcendent is the breadth and intelligence of her observations, and her ability to not simply describe how Italy looks and smells, but how its sunlight feels, what emotions its churches and boulevards evoke, what its people believe and pray for and fear. Ms. Harrison's descriptions aspire not to the precision of postcards, but to the richness of dream. In this, *Italian Days* succeeds almost too well: I sometimes wonder if Ms. Harrison's conjured version of Italy has subconsciously replaced my own memories. It's not that my memories are faded, it's that her Italy seems truer than mine. *Italian Days* doesn't just reflect Italy; it creates it. ✧

RECOMMENDATION
PLANT LIFE by Pamela Duncan

Lynn Pruett

It is rare that a talent as fine as Pamela Duncan's illuminates working-class lives. *Plant Life*, her second novel, is a refreshing portrayal of women who work in the Revel textile mill in Russell, North Carolina. With beautiful, dignified prose and just the right touch of humor, Duncan avoids both a grim political account and the all-too-common comic/grotesque/violent tale literary working-class Southerners seem doomed to inhabit. Instead *Plant Life* recalls Harriette Arnow's *The Dollmaker* and James Still's *River of Earth*, whose characters have a great desire to change circumstances, but biology, economics, and social expectations block their paths.

The novel begins in Las Vegas with Laurel Granger, who left the mill town for college and a marriage that eventually turned sour. Stunned and divorced, she returns to Russell and takes the only job she can find as secretary in the plant's office. Unexpected romances come her way as she reassesses her place in the world. The best discovery occurs when, as a member of the plant's work force, she joins her mother's lifelong friends in the lunchroom. These gatherings are wonderful scenes. Tensions ripple through the marvelous dialogue as Pansy, Percilla, Maxann, Idalene, and Lottie Mae exchange sandwiches and opinions. Eventually each woman tells her story, and we learn how complicated this knot of relationships is and that unacknowledged blood kinships create the most vociferous antagonisms in the group.

The harshest, most haunting, and intimate voice is that of the deceased Alberta (Bert) Dill, Laurel's grandmother, who was denied education despite her fertile mind and gift for language. As a result of her stunting, the Depression, eight children, and a disappointing marriage, Bert's actions, shocking and cruel, are the most dramatic act of mother love she performs. She says,

> Many a time I wished I could have cut out that part of my heart that refused to be satisfied . . . Sometimes it's better to stay ignorant and not know what else is out there in the world, what all you might like but won't never get to have for yourself.

It's from Bert's and Pansy's twined stories that the reader comes to understand the damage of poverty. It is not a lack of intelligence or artistic ability that prevents the brightest in rural towns from escaping to cities or universities, but a lack of opportunity and support for the radical notion of postponing a paycheck in order to develop the mind. Laurel's return challenges all simple formulas for happiness and success both in Russell and in the world beyond.

Charting the turbulence and beauty of daily life, *Plant Life* continues in the domain of Duncan's delightful debut novel, *Moon Women*. ✧

ANTARCTICA by Claire Keegan

Michael Lowenthal

Last summer I had the privilege of staying at the Hawthornden Castle Retreat for Writers in Scotland. Hawthornden is owned by Mrs. Drue Heinz, the publisher of *The Paris Review*, and the castle's library includes the back issues of that venerable journal—which, I'll admit, I had always admired more than actually read. I decided to rectify that situation, and so every day for a month I took a different copy of the journal into my room at lunch time and read whatever caught my eye.

One story slammed me so hard I would swear I saw stars. I had never heard of its author, but as soon as I returned home I looked her up and found that she had published one book, a collection of stories. I bought it immediately and gobbled it in a day. The story was "The Singing Cashier," its author is the Irish writer Claire Keegan, and her book is *Antarctica* (Grove Press, 2001).

"The Singing Cashier" has fangs, and they bite from the very first line: "Smethers, the postman, that greasy fuck with his brown letters." (God bless a writer with the guts to name a slimy character Smethers! And to begin a story with a verbless sentence fragment!) The story is narrated by an Irish teenager who lives with her older sister, Cora. Their parents are dead, so Cora is trying to support them both with her job as a grocery-store cashier, but they need all the help they can get; when the postman Smethers starts bringing parcels of fish along with the mail, Cora invites him in. Listen to the startling slantwise economy of Keegan's writing:

> My no-nonsense sister puts up with him. She needs his smelly parcels, I suppose, and cups of tea are cheap enough . . . It's Wednesday, and we're down to the last few tea bags, so the cups will be peppered with dust today. Smethers sits down snug in the armchair. Cora turns on the radio, tunes into Jimmy Young, who's giving things away. Then she wriggles a coin out of her purse and hands it over.
> "Will you go down and get me a box of matches?"
> "Matches? But there's —"
> "Piss off now, there's a love."
> She gives me the "Just do it" look, so I stomp down to the newsagent's in Breswill Street, a good ten-minute walk each way, but I come home too soon and notice Smethers's belt is notched up tight and Cora's nightdress is inside out, her hands fidgeting with the fuzz around her slipper. And the smell, like sleep gone sticky. Oatmeal boiled over.

That last paragraph has to be the most painfully vivid sex-scene-in-absentia I've ever come across.

I won't give away the rest of the story, but it involves the revelation that a neighbor—a friend of their dead father's—has been murdering teenage girls on their street. The story is brutal and sad and tender . . . and all in less than eight pages.

If all of the stories in *Antarctica* don't rise to quite this level, many come very, very close. Even when Keegan is not spot-on, she is in the front ranks of originality in terms of both the stories she chooses to tell and the language in which she tells them. Her quirky, headstrong voice, even in this first young book, is decisively her own.

The title story, "Antarctica," is another stunner. A "happily married woman" takes the train into the city one December weekend to see what it feels like to sleep with another man. She promptly meets one who subverts her (and readers') expectations, and then, in a brilliantly creepy series of turns, subverts the subversion. I don't want to say more, but it's the kind of story that makes you fear deeply for its author: anyone capable of dreaming up a situation, and a character, like this must spend a great deal of time in the abyss. The bleak chill of the story's final paragraph makes Antarctica itself seem like a tropical paradise.

My other favorite stories are another about two sisters ("Sisters") and another about adultery ("Love in the Tall Grass"). The best writers tend to worry the same obsessions again and again.

Keegan writes with equal adeptness about Ireland and America, women and men, city and countryside. Her stories inspire all the tooth-buzzing suspense of horror films, but the suspense is as much about emotion as it is about plot: she has us on the edge of our seats waiting to find out exactly when and in what manner her characters' hearts will be broken.

But in that curious and thrilling paradox effected by good literature, reading about their broken hearts somehow begins to mend our own. ✧

Robert Walser

Kevin Canty

Pedestrian is an odd word. We don't mean anything kind when we apply it to someone. Pedestrian crossings slow us down in our exciting automotive adventures. Pedestrian movies, pedestrian meals, pedestrian conversation are all odious.

And yet the greatest pedestrian in literary history, Robert Walser, is back in print and ready to be rediscovered again. In stories like "A Little Ramble" and "The Walk" and "The Little Tree" Walser ventures out into the world on foot, at a walker's pace, and reflects and reports on what he finds there. Sometimes it is his own fancy, as in "The Man With the Pumpkin Head" or "Stork and Hedgehog," a dialog which begins:

> HEDGEHOG: Aren't I captivating? Tell me.
> STORK: For a long time I have loved you.

and ends:

> How the stork would have loved to kiss, with his beak, the spines of the hedgehog. What a kissing that would have been! We shudder at the thought of it.

More often, though, he seems to find something in the world to notice, something we might have passed by: a little tree, a woman wearing trousers, a French newspaper. Out of these he would make what he called "little Walserings"—confections of language disguised as stories, though none of them have a plot, exactly. Nor for the most part are they prose poems, exactly. He doesn't seem to have any ancestors or any descendants or even any close cousins; he stands off to one side of literary history, watching and musing.

Like Musil, Kafka, Hamsun, his central character (is there more than one?) is a failure—not only a social and financial failure but a metaphysical failure as well. Not only does he have nothing, he is nothing; or rather he is one thing here and another thing there, a dissociated scatter of selves. What sets the Walser character apart from Gregor Samsa or Malte Laurids Brigge is his ease and good cheer. He doesn't seem to mind. Success would be in bad taste, a little ostentatious, a little showy. A fixed, stable, integrated self could be secured only by sacrificing these other flighty selves. And where would the fun be in that? It is this lightness and love of the world that brings me back to Walser's writing, once or twice a year, just for the pleasure of his company.

A word or two about the writer's life is probably in order, though—like so many twentieth-century literary all-stars—it makes for depressing reading. He lived in poverty and obscurity, though he did publish a book in his lifetime. He grew increasingly eccentric—his last works, which he called microscripts, were written in tiny writing in tiny squares in the middle of a blank page, a struggle between speech and silence which the silence eventually won. After a suicide attempt in 1929 he checked himself into an institution, where his depression was misdiagnosed as schizophrenia. From 1933 until his death in 1956 there was no more writing; "I did not come here to write," he said of the institution, "I came here to be mad." He died of a heart attack while on a walk in the snow on Christmas Day, after a silence that lasted 23 years.

The very peculiar thing about this life is how little it seems to be reflected in his work. The stories, in their endless experiment, their willingness to come at life from every angle, strike me as the work of a confident, playful mind. I don't know what it was like to be Walser when he was not at work, but when he was writing he was swimming, not drowning. Listen to a few of these first lines and tell me different:

A she-owl in a ruined wall said to herself: what a horrifying existence "The She-Owl".

Kienast was the name of a man who wanted nothing to do with anything "Kienast".

I am a little worn out, raddled, squashed, downtrodden, shot full of holes "Nervous".

The three people, the captain, a gentleman, and a young girl, climb into the basket, the anchoring chords are loosed, and the strange house flies, slowly, as if it had first to ponder something, upward "Balloon Journey".

These stories lurch into motion with the first line and never look back—eccentric motion, certainly, but carefully controlled, deeply original, and interesting. Walser will take you places no other writer will.

The place to start is the *Selected Stories*, back in print from the New York Review Books Classics, 42 little trips into the unknown and sometimes back, in lucid, graceful translations, mostly by Christopher Middleton. The second stop would be the novel *Jakob von Gunten*, also in print, which was actually made into a movie a few years ago by the brothers Quay. But do start, before he disappears again. He will never be major; he wouldn't want to be major, it would go against the grain, it would be presumptuous—but he will always be himself, alone, on foot, walking, noticing things we didn't notice, seeing what we can't see. ✧

OPEN DOORS by Leonardo Sciascia

Peter Orner

I'd like to recommend the novella "Death and the Knight" by the Italian novelist Leonardo Sciascia. It appears in a book of Sciascia's novellas called *Open Doors*. An odd story about a police deputy investigating a murder case—but for me it's more a meditation on power and helplessness. At one point a character—who himself will soon be murdered says:

> There is one power, which is visible, identifiable, and numerable, but there is another, which is without name or without names, and which swims underwater. The visible power is in permanent conflict with the underwater power, especially at the moments when it has the gall to break the surface with vigor, that is to say with violence and bloodshed . . .

Of course, the quote could be interpreted as an angle on the mafia in Italy and Sciascia is famous for his many books on Sicily and the mafia but this late story reaches into far murkier areas and is, finally, more about the mind than killing. The police deputy is a man buried under a lifetime of reading. Not a clichéd bookish cop, but someone literally paralyzed by memories of what he's read, even at one point confusing a description from a Gadda novel with something he's lived through himself. The story's initial murder has something to do with one of the most powerful businessmen in Italy—a man called simply "The President," but the police investigation centers on a mythical terrorist group invented to obscure The President's involvement. The deputy sees—not for the first time —that the truth will never come out because no one is particularly interested in it. And worse, the idea of it is frightening to most people. And yet, and yet . . . the deputy, perhaps due in some way to his obsession withliterature, insists, to the end, that he has no choice but to continue his lonely (and suicidal) quest to link The President to the murder. He says to a journalist—as equally uninterested in what actually happened as his boss on the police force —"Have you ever heard of the love of truth?" The journalist answers: "Vaguely." It's a dark story—and strange (we remain in the head of the deputy, but with frequent asides that keep a reader way off-balance)—by a writer who should be far more read in the U.S. than he is. ✧

Michael Byers and THE COAST OF GOOD INTENTIONS

Roy Parvin

By all rights, I should have come to know of Michael Byers sooner. Both of us in the mid-nineties had a story within the covers of the same anthology. For a period of time, too, we lived in the same part of the world, San Francisco, and shared a number of writer friends, but somehow our paths never crossed.

It wasn't until the publication of *The Coast of Good Intentions* in the early spring of 1998 that his work made a lasting impression. I'd moved north to the top shelf of California by then, to the deep woods, was hard at work on the novella that would eventually become the title story of my second book. At the time, the piece was resisting my best efforts to tell it, embarrassing even now to admit how many countless, fruitless pages I'd thrown at it. The nearest bookstore was—and still is—a sixty-mile roundtrip, a long way to go for a book, though I would have gladly driven twice the distance that particular afternoon to escape my own leaden narrative.

I returned home with *The Coast of Good Intentions* and promptly devoured the collection of stories like food. There are so many things that recommend the book—the music of the language; the unerring ear for dialogue; the sense of real life captured on the page—but what struck me more than anything else at the time was Byers's confidence to slow the stories down, to let each run by its own internal clock, avoiding the trap of the headlong rush to the big ending or revealing epiphany, the all-too-creaky fictional device where, as Charles Baxter calls it, "the world of appearances falls away, and essences show themselves." What Byers's stories turn on is character rather than circumstance and, as such, resist easy summation. He writes of carpenters and geologists, park rangers and computer programmers: people struggling for footing after divorce or death or disappointment. If there's any common ground from one story to the next, it's the misty Pacific Northwest backdrop and the fumbling hopefulness of ordinary people who've been knocked about by life but still try to find some better fit for themselves, a place that more rightfully could be deemed home. What's extraordinary is how much nuance Byers invests in these everyday struggles. Without any unnecesary palaver or intrusive psychoanalyzing, we're able to understand his characters down to the marrow.

In the end, any good story can only be reduced so far. You can attempt to take it apart like a watchmaker to find out precisely how it ticks, but ultimately only pieces of the animating mechanism can be divined. You hit a chunk that cannot be categorized or broken down. It's organic, seemingly not the product of invention, but as if it always existed. It simply is—the work of Alice Munro or Rick Bass immediately comes to mind as serviceable examples. For my money, that undigested chunk of a good story is where magic or art resides, and, in that regard, the stories in *The Coast of Good Intentions* are very chunky indeed. Where in the world did Byers get the idea for a character to write a play about Mary Stilwell, Thomas Edison's lesser-known first wife? Or, in another story, to combine elements of opera, promiscuous children, and a widower who makes an ill-fated pass at his mother-in-law? Impossible to guess. I've pressed this book into the hands of more colleagues than I could count, and each has evinced a similar wonder to my own. I've recommended it as well to non-writer friends—civilians—and the response there has been mixed; they find the stories depressing, or more precisely, not happy. But, of course, happy isn't the assignment, and I suspect that in their blind pursuit of Hollywood endings, they miss entirely the quiet grace that suffuses each story. Or it could just be that Byers falls within the category of writers' writer.

That afternoon that I drove out of the woods to the bookstore back in 1998 was the first day I was able to find my way out of the thickets of my own many revisions. *The Coast of Good Intentions* gave me the courage to slow down, to locate the story in the small moments on every single page. ✧

TRUE GRIT by Charles Portis

Tom Franklin

A novel one shouldn't ever read in the middle of trying to write a novel is Charles Portis's *True Grit*. Over the last four years I've been struggling to complete my first novel, *Hell at the Breech*, and made the above mistake. I'd been writing in all third person, and was so stunned by the clarity, the humor, the personality in Portis's narrator's first-person voice that I immediately began my novel (which had been well over four hundred pages long) over.

You'd think a thirty-eight-year-old man who'd been writing for twenty years would be beyond imitation, but *True Grit's* vision is so pure, Mattie Ross's voice so memorable, that I was suddenly writing bad—very bad— Portis. I did about fifty pages of this before giving up and returning to my original pages, saddened that I'd never write a book anywhere near as good as Portis.

When most of us hear *True Grit*, we think of the very good John Wayne movie based on the novel. But when you read the book, you realize that most of the dialogue is lifted right out of Portis's pages. Listen to what Rooster Cogburn tells Mattie Ross:

> My wife did not crave the society of my river friends. She got a bellyful of it and decided she would go back to her first husband who was clerking in a hardware over in Paducah. She said, 'Goodbye, Reuben, a love for decency does not abide in you.' There is your divorced woman talking about decency. I told her, I said, 'Goodbye, Nola, I hope that little nail-selling bastard will make you happy this time.' She took my boy with her too. He never did like me anyhow. I guess I did speak awful rough to him but I didn't mean nothing by it. You would not want to see a clumsier child than Horace. I bet he broke forty cups.

Beyond the dialogue, though, is Mattie's narration, itself a wondrous thing to behold. She has the delightful habit of placing quotation marks around anything she considers to be a colloquialism. For example: I knew they were up to some "stunt." By the time I was a few pages in, I was laughing out loud at this habit. These quotations accrue and help to paint a vivid picture of the spinster telling her story many years later. The best thing about this book, perhaps, is the feeling that, behind this story, there is a real life. Charles Portis's most memorable character is not, then, Rooster Cogburn, but his narrator, Mattie Ross.

I can't recommend this novel highly enough. One should also read Portis's other books, especially his first, *Norwood*. ✧

Three Australian Novelists

Sabina Murray

True History of the Kelly Gang by Peter Carey
Gould's Book of Fish by Richard Flanagan
The Chant of Jimmie Blacksmith by Thomas Keneally

As of late, I have found myself wanting a book full of outlaws who terrorize the (corrupt/tyrannical/despotic) powers that be. Perhaps I'm not the only reader in this disposition. With this in mind, I have three books to recommend, all Australian. Despite the fact that the population of Australia is composed mostly of twentieth century immigrant waves, most recently the Vietnamese, the Australia that has entered the western consciousness is that of British convict colony. Because of this, the Australian national identity is one that has formed in opposition to authority and that owes much to the rise of the bushranger hero, a frequent figure in traditional Australian narratives, folksongs, and lately some impressive and moving fiction.

The first book I would like to recommend is the *True History of the Kelly Gang*, by Peter Carey. Winner of a Booker prize (Carey's second, his first was for *Oscar and Lucinda*), *The Kelly Gang* creates a disturbing reality out of colonial Victoria in the late nineteenth century. Carey treads dangerous territory in a number of ways. Firstly, he writes from the first person point of view of an intelligent man whose education is limited. What could be an annoying, broken narrative becomes—with Carey's fine writing—seductive and convincing. Secondly, by writing the fierce bushranger as a sympathetic character, Ned Kelly could have become victim to the maudlin along with the colonial government. But Ned Kelly comes to us as a complicated, reasonable, brave man, which is just how I like my heroes. As a child, growing up in Australia, my friends and I used to run around with paper bags on our heads (a nod to Kelly's primitive armor) having a go at being Ned Kelly. We terrorized our teachers. Somehow, Carey's book remains loyal to this spirit.

A wonderful read of the last year is Richard Flanagan's *Gould's Book of Fish*. Full of imagery, Flanagan's Sarah Island—a place resounding with the screams of a thousand mistreated convicts and running with their blood—becomes a place of difficult beauty. Once more, we are cheering the convicts and wishing their tormentors all manner of painful ills. And although *Book of Fish* keeps you in its slippery grasp until the end, the book turns out to be much more than a fish tale. I found myself wondering not only about Australia's convict past, but also about the nature of art, narrative, and history.

I would also like to recommend Thomas (yes, he did write *Schindler's List*) Keneally's *The Chant of Jimmie Blacksmith* of 1972. Jimmie Blacksmith is the son of a white man and an aborigine mother. Based on a true account of one man's murderous rampage in 1900, *The Chant of Jimmie Blacksmith* is a gripping, disturbing read. Although I did not find myself cheering Blacksmith through the various horrors he inflicts, I did understand him to be the product of an oppressive reality, one in which he might have been forgotten had he not written himself—in blood—into history.

Those are my recommendations, but if you find yourself with an extra couple of weeks and some space in your suitcase, I have very much enjoyed reading the books of Tim Winton, a Western Australian writer, and also *Eucalyptus* by Murray Bail, which might be the perfect gift for that friend of yours with a tree fetish. ✧

ET CETERA | POST ROAD

Lolita A-Z

Zoran Kuzmanovich with Vic Brand, Brigand Green, Meredith Greer,
Denise Hernandez, Sarah Holden, Christian Hunt, Heather Larson, Jennifer
Lyon, Matthew McKillop, Jason McMullan, Derrick Miller, Mary Louise
Ryan, Marshall Stuckey, Britton Taylor.

"*Lolita* A-Z" was conceived as the first in a series of exercises in annotation
designed to explore the depths and expose the pitfalls of intertexuality
theory for the 1997 version of English 473: Joyce/Nabokov Seminar, a
course I offer roughly every other year at Davidson College. Almost all
members of the seminar had read *Lolita* before taking the course but
found fairly demanding the close-reading of Nabokov's problematic,
playful and polyglot text. To enjoy their romp on the lexical playfields
these students made full use of the reference resources at the Davidson
College's Little Library and its librarians, especially Mrs. Sharon Byrd.
After I annotated a number of entries to establish the pattern, the group
was guided by a single principle: they wanted to create a resource that
they wished they had had as they read *Lolita* for the first time. With a view
towards future editions of the seminar, they agreed to put aside the thor-
oughly well researched and densely printed 138 pages of notes in Alfred
Appel Jr.'s *The Annotated Lolita* as having done too much discovering for
them and instead adopted as a model the Oxford University Press/Facts
on File A-Z series. Knowing that anyone already familiar with Nabokov
would find any single reference work on *Lolita* unlikely to encompass
everything about the book, they nonetheless supplied information that is
well beyond the appetites of the beginning reader. Since 1997, the "reading-
as-annotation" assignment has acquired a life of its own, and now "*Lolita*
A-Z" is a part of a larger series of quick but useful web-based and thus
revisable annotations for each of Nabokov's major works. Eventually
these annotations will form a larger project Nabokov A-Z that would
include biographical and critical as well as explicative materials. All page
references are to the Vintage International edition of *Lolita*.

Ahnaten, King of Egypt: With Queen Nefertiti had seven, not six daughters.

Arlesienne: A popular painting of Vincent van Gogh's (1853-1890) widely
reproduced in America and originally painted in 1888. The title refers
to the subject of the portrait, a woman from the town of Arles in
Provence, France.

Auteuil: A city in France where Humbert teaches English to a group
of adults.

Aunt Clare: The fictitious name Humbert leaves with Mr. Swine
(Humbert mistakenly refers to him as Mr. Swoon, another lodger at The
Enchanted Hunters) to have his wife call. This is to continue the ruse that
Charlotte is alive and should be calling for him and Dolores. It is also Nabokov's
way of dangling the thread of Quilty's presence for the careful reader.

Aztec Red Convertible: The first in a series of cars which began following Humbert and Lolita after they left the Beardsley school. Also referred to as the Red Yak; Humbert initially believes the car is driven by a detective he names Detective Trapp. In his paranoic state, Humbert believes this detective is following them to decipher the truth behind Humbert's relationship with Lolita.

Bagration Island: Folio compiled by Melanie Weiss containing over 800 pictures of penises; the book is offered to Humbert by Clare Quilty while trying to bargain for his life.

Bailey, Benjamin: (1791-1853) The friend to whom Keats sent letters about his poetic theories. Humbert publishes an article on the Proustian theme of those letters.

Barbara: Lolita went rowing with her while at Camp Q. Her sister was the camp Waterfront Director.

Basque: An obscure language spoken by the largely bilingual Basques that has been largely replaced by French and Spanish. Humbert describes one of the nurses in the hospital as being of Basque descent, and he believes he is being plotted against in an obscure language such as Basque or Zemfirian so that he might be kept from Lolita.

Beale, Frederick Jr.: Driver of the black Packard that strikes and kills Charlotte Haze.

Beard, Miss: A woman looking for Dr. Braddock at The Enchanted Hunters. Quite a name for a lady.

Beardsley, Aubrey (Vincent): The name of Humbert and Lolita's college town serves as Nabokov's tribute to Vincent Beardsley (1872-1898), the English illustrator of the late Victorian era. After Oscar Wilde, he was the major figure in the Aestheticism movement. Over the course of his lifetime he provided artwork for such pieces as Wilde's *Salome*, and Malory's *Morte d'Arthur* as well as illustrations for editions of *Volpone*, *Lysistrata*, *The Rape of the Lock*, and *Under the Hill*. Much of his work was considered decadent, even scandalous for his time. He enjoyed erotic art as he garnered a special liking for painting excessively large sexual organs.

Beardsley: The college town to which Humbert and Lolita retire. It has three major educational fixtures: the first is a girls' day school, which Humbert hopes will be a "high-class, non-coeducational one, with no modern nonsense," but which turns out to be more similar to a "finishing school." The second is the Beardsley College for Women. The third is Butler Academy.

Beauté Humaine, La: Pichon's anatomy book Humbert investigates while his father is away.

Belleau, Remy: (1528-1577) A poet of the French Renaissance; a quotation from his poem (with a reference to the female genitals) appears in Humbert's journal.

Bert: A photographer on the Arctic Canada expedition who has highly colored dreams.

Bill, a.k.a. Discreet Bill: The Schillers' neighbor at their Hunter Road residence; he lost his arm in Italy during World War II. He is helping Dick fix things in the yard when he makes his appearance, and later hurts his thumb whilst opening beers.

Bird, Avis: Her name means "Bird" Bird. She is the "heavy, unattractive, affectionate child" (285) for whom Dolores feels jealousy because of Avis' pure, unsexualized relationship with her father, Mr. Bird.

Bluebeard: The murderous husband in a fairy tale by Charles Perrault.

Bosch, Hieronymus: A fifteenth-century Dutch painter whose works are characterized by grotesque, fantastic creatures mingling with human figures. Humbert describes Lolita playing doubles on the tennis court: "She moved like a fair angel among three horrible Boschian cripples" (235).

Botticelli's Venus: *The Birth of Venus*, a painting by Sandro Botticelli (1445-1510), depicts a modest Venus rising from the sea on a pastel-pink shell. Dolores is described as having "always looked like Botticelli's russet Venus, the same soft nose, the same blurred beauty" (270). The later reference to Lo's "Florentine breasts" (274) is also an evocation of this Venus.

Boyd, Dr.: Gave a talk while Humbert and Lolita were staying at The Enchanted Hunters.

Braddock, Mr., Dr.: Humbert is mistaken for this man at The Enchanted Hunters.

Brewster, Jack: A telephone worker that Clare Quilty mistakes Humbert for when Humbert comes to kill him. Jack has a brother with the same telephone company.

Briceland: Town in which The Enchanted Hunters is located.

Broughton, Hugh: (1549-1612) Puritan divine with an interest in Biblical chronology.

Browning, Robert: Humbert refers to, or quotes, Browning as he describes Lolita picking her dress out from her "peach-cleft." He went sixty miles to buy Browning's *Dramatic Works* among other books to take to Lolita in the hospital the last time that he goes to see her.

Burke, Barbara: Girl at Camp Q who was two years older than Dolores and the best swimmer. She had intercourse behind a bush with Charlie Holmes every morning of July while Dolores stood watch, and finally Dolores decided to try it, too.

Butler Academy for Boys: A single-sex day school in Beardsley.

Camp Q: The camp where Dolores Haze goes the summer before her thirteenth birthday. Wake-up call is at 6:30 every morning. Also site where Lolita first had sexual intercourse.

Canada: Humbert went on an ill-defined expedition to Arctic Canada (with an ambiguous goal) with the brother of one of his psychologists. Here he experienced an abeyance in his lust for nymphets.

Catullus: Little is known about the personal life of Gaius Valerius Catullus, a Latin poet who lived approximately from 84-54 BC He is known for his fervent lyric poetry, dedicated to his mistress Lesbia, and such pieces have been imitated by a myriad of English poets. For Catullus, Lesbia was an obsession, and his love for her became his religion. He is also said to be the precursor to Ovid, and to the medieval tradition of courtly love.

Central Park: Where Humbert tries to find nymphets while living in New York City.

Champion, Colorado: Where Humbert takes Lolita after leaving the Beardsley School. Humbert feels safe there because no one from the school has telephoned, and no one knows he's there; they think he is in Hollywood.

Champion Hotel: The hotel where Humbert and Lolita spend the night when they stay in Champion, Colorado.

Chapman, Avis: One of Lolita's friends at the Beardsley School for Girls: a "plump, lateral" child with "hairy legs."

Chateaubriandesque: A reference to Francois Rene de Chateaubriand, a French writer considered a forerunner of Romanticism.

Chatfield, Mrs.: The mother of Phyllis Chatfield; attendant at the Murphy-Fantasia wedding who accosts Humbert in order to engage him in small talk.

Chatfield, Phyllis: Daughter of Mrs. Chatfield; takes turns with Dolores Haze and Barbara Burke having sex with Charlie Holmes at Camp Q.

***Children-Colors*:** A play written by Clare Quilty and Vivian Darkbloom. Lolita sees a performance of the play at the Magic Cave. Humbert believes the idea of the play originated from James Joyce. The play involves young girls portraying the colors of the rainbow. Humbert is especially excited by the girls portraying Orange and Emerald.

***Children's Encyclopedia*:** Humbert looks through it in the prison library for the photos of Girl Scouts.

Chum: Humbert's nickname for his .32 caliber handgun that he uses to kill Clare Quilty.

Clark, Clarence Choate, Esq.: Humbert's lawyer (District of Columbia), passes on to John Ray, Jr., Humbert's manuscript. Ray is Clark's good friend and relation.

Confession of a White Widowed Male: The original subtitle given to Humbert's manuscript.

Coalmont: The industrial town where Dolores Haze has taken up residence with her husband, Richard Schiller.

Cooper, Dr.: He interrupts Humbert and Annabel.

Corfu: A Greek island where Annabel Leigh dies of typhus.

Corn Palace: The Corn Palace is located in Mitchell, South Dakota. It was first constructed in 1892 as a tribute to Mitchell's farmland. The building's exterior is currently decorated with 3,000 bushels of corn in addition to its Moorish minarets and towers.

Crater Lake: Located in southern Oregon on the crest of the southern Cascade Range. The lake lies in a crater created by a volcano and is 6 miles in diameter, 26 miles in circumference. Crater Lake and the area surrounding were declared a National Park in 1902.

Cyrano de Bergerac, Savinien: A seventeenth-century French satirist and dramatist whose life became the basis of many romantic legends, the most famous of which is Edmond Rostand's play *Cyrano de Bergerac.* In this play, he is portrayed as a lover who is intelligent and charming but shy and ugly and in possession of a very large nose. One of Lolita's acting drills includes "palpat[ing] the face of" such figures as Cyrano's, with its very large nose. Lola's acting drills are one of the things that Humbert loves to watch.

Dahl, Mona: The "elegantly evasive" non-nymphettish friend of Lolita's with an I.Q. of 150 and a preference for the company of Marines.

Dante: Born in 1265, Dante met Beatrice in 1274 when she was eight. Figure it out.

Darkbloom, Vivian: An anagram for Vladimir Nabokov. The author of *My Cue,* a biography. Collaborator with Clare Quilty in *The Lady Who Loved Lightning.* Also co-authors the play *Children-Colors* with Clare Quilty.

de R., Mme: The woman who accompanies Humbert's father to Italy in the summer of 1923.

de Ronsard, Pierre: (1524-1585) A prominent French Renaissance poet quoted in Humbert's journal; the quote is in praise of female genitalia: "oh little red slit."

Death Valley: The lowest point in the western hemisphere (9282 feet below sea level) and one of the hottest places on Earth. A desert basin in southeastern California and parts of Nevada, Death Valley bears its name from the gold prospectors who perished there in the years following the 1849 gold rush. The Death Valley National Monument, with an area of nearly 3,000 square miles, was established in 1933.

Deux Magots: (Two Monkeys) The famous Paris cafe on the Left Bank, hospitable to the likes of Jean Paul Sartre and Ernest Hemingway. Neither writer is a favorite of Nabokov's.

Dietrich, Marlene: A German actress who was popular in the 1930s and whom Humbert believes Mrs. Haze resembles.

"Do the Senses make Sense?": An article by John Ray Jr. on morbid states and perversions. It has won the Poling Prize.

Duk Duk Ranch: The sex farm a day's drive from Elphinstone at which Clare Quilty sets up camp for the summer. The ranch belongs to the brother of the red-headed man with whom Lo plays tennis on page 234. It burned mysteriously to the ground sometime after Lo and Fay left the ranch in disgust.

East, Miss: Humbert's designation for his "east-door" neighbor on Thayer St. in Beardsley, whose single and apparently innocent conversation with Lolita earns Humbert's lasting distrust. (The western neighbor is designated as "Mr. West.")

Edith, Mlle: A madam in Paris whorehouse Humbert visits.

Elphinstone: The town in Colorado, "a gem of a western State," where Humbert takes Lolita and loses her forever.

Enchanted Hunters, The: The hotel in Briceland where Humbert and Dolores stay after he picks her up from camp. A religious convention clashing with a flower show in Briceland forces the hotel to give away Humbert's twin-bedded room at half past six resulting in a double bed room for the "father/daughter" combination. And the site where Humbert and Dolores first have sexual intercourse.

Eskimos: Indigenous poeples of Arctic coastal regions in North America, Greenland, and N. Siberia; sometimes considered Native Americans. Humbert encounters Eskimos on the expedition to Arctic Canada and has no desire for the little Eskimo girls with "guinea pig" faces and fish smells.

Fabian, Miss: A suggestively named "fadedly feminine" neighbor of Humbert's on Thayer St. in Beardsley, and a professor of English at Beardsley College. See also Miss Lester.

Farlow, John and Jean: Neighbors of the Hazes who look after Charlotte's "meager estate" after her death. Humbert convinces John that Lolita is his natural child; a fear of disillusioning him dissuades Humbert from seeking John's legal advice when his guardianship of Lolita is called into question.

Farson: A city in southwestern Wyoming, located approximately 60 miles from Pinedale.

Fascinum: An ivory penis used in ancient cults' erotic rituals.

Fatamorganas: Mirages Humbert hopes for once he and Lolita cross the border with Mexico.

Galsworthy, John: British novelist, essayist, and playwright (1867-1933). He won the Nobel Prize for Literature in 1932 and is known for *The Forsyte Saga*, a collection of novels tracing the history of the Forsyte family. Galsworthy often explored the interests of Victorian and Edwardian society, and his novels often delved into the subject of man's passion for possession.

Girl Scout Motto: The Girl Scout Promise is: On my honor, I will try: To serve God and my country, To help people at all times, And to live by the Girl Scout Law. This may have been changed since Lolita's childhood.

Godin, Gaston: A professor in the French department of the Beardsley College for Women; he uses Humbert's textbook in his classes and once attempts to get him to deliver a lecture there. A grossly overweight immigrant from France with a poor command of English and few scholarly skills, he is nevertheless fawned over by the faculty and residents of Beardsley. His sexual predilection is for young boys. Humbert frequently plays chess with Gaston, and beats him. Humbert says that he could see stratagems through the board, as though the board were a pool of water, and that Gaston was unable to see them.

Gold, Edusa: Humbert coincidentaly pulls up beside this striking woman at a traffic signal as he takes off from Beardsley School with Lolita. Edusa is apparently Lolita's tennis coach at Beardsley. Lolita was about to be in a play at the school, and Edusa expresses disappointment that Humbert has taken her out of it, saying that Lolita was a wonderful actress.

Gold, Electra: Edusa's sister, who is also a tennis coach. In Greek mythology, Electra, with her brother Orestes, avenged their father (Agamemnon) by killing their mother (Clytemnestra) and her lover (Aegisthus). Also another reference to Freudian psychology; a daughter's unconscious desire for her father.

Grammar, G. Edward: "a thirty-five-year-old New York office manager who had just been arrayed on a charge of murdering his thirty-three-year-old wife, Dorothy" (287). He bludgeoned his wife and sent her battered body careening down the street in their car. He was caught when the authorities realized that the bruises on Dorothy's body did not match the damage to the car.

Gray Star: A settlement in the "remotest" Northwest.

Grimm Road: In Parkington, the address of Clare Quilty's ancestral home, Pavor Manor.

Hall, Linda: One of Lolita's companions at the Beardsley School for Girls. She is the school tennis champion; Humbert suspects she is a "true nymphet," but Lolita never allows him to have any contact with her.

Hamilton, Mary Rose: "Dark" friend of Lolita.

Harry Edgar: Edgar Allan Poe.

Haze, Mrs. Charlotte: The mother of Lolita. She is a typical bourgeois woman in her middle thirties; she is versed in soulless, vacuous parlor talk and is a thrall to the rules of etiquette and women's book club "refinement." She attempts and fails to speak French, is highly critical of Lolita's "inproperness," and is attracted to the "exotic" European Humbert who is a lodger in her house.

Haze, Dolores: See Lolita.

Haze, Mr. Harold: Charlotte's previous husband and real father of Dolores.

Hells Canyon: Formed by the Snake River on the Idaho-Oregon boundary, Hells Canyon is the deepest gorge in North America. The total length of the canyon stretches over 125 miles; its depth reaches a maximum of 7,900 feet. Hells Canyon and the area surrounding were declared a national recreational area in 1975.

Herr Doktor Humbert: Humbert refers to himself as he ponders creating a "healthy" girlhood for Lolita.

***Histoire abrégé de la poésie anglaise*:** Humbert's book *Short History of English Poetry*.

Holigan, Mrs.: A maid whose services Humbert inherits from the previous tenants at his residence on Thayer St. in Beardsley. She is inobservant enough to miss the signs of Humbert's relationship with Lolita.

Holmes, Charlie: The sullen thirteen year old son of Camp Q's mistress with whom Barbara Burke, Phyllis Chatfield, and Dolores have intercourse by turns behind a bush while supposedly carrying a boat to the nearby lakes. Some time later, Humbert finds out in his final return to Ramsdale that Charlie was killed in Korea.

Holmes, Ms.: The "camp mistress" of Camp Q.

Hotel Mirana: A hotel on the French Riviera. Humbert meets Annabel Leigh there.

Horner, Sally: An eleven-year-old alleged molestation victim of Frank Lasalle, a fifty-year-old mechanic.

Hourglass Lake: The lake where Humbert and Charlotte go to swim and sunbathe while Lolita is away at camp. It is also where Humbert first learns of Charlotte's plans for sending Lolita to boarding school, and where he first contemplates killing Charlotte.

Edgar, H. Humbert, Dr.: False name Humbert uses at The Enchanted Hunters. The name extends the veil of references to Edgar Allan Poe.

Humbert Humbert: Also H.H., Humberg, Humbug, Herbert, Herr Doktor Humbert, Dr. Edgar H. Humbert, Jean-Jacques Humbert. Author of *Lolita, or the Confession of a White Widowed Male*; died in legal custody of a broken heart on November 16,1952, while awaiting trial for a crime reported upon in the daily papers for September 1952 (killing Clare Quilty). Born in 1910 in Paris. Of Swiss, French, and Austrian ancestry. Has a theory of nymphetdoom (or nymphetdom). Likes to create false dreams to deceive psychologists; highly critical of psychoanalysis.

Hunter Road: The home (last one at the end of the street) of Dolores and Richard Schiller in which Humbert finally confronts the runaway Lo and gets from her the name of the villain who seduced her away from him in Elphinstone: Clare Quilty.

Insomnia Lodge: Humbert's nickname for the Parkington hotel where he spent a sleepless night before killing Clare Quilty.

Jean Christophe: A ten-volume novel by Romain Rolland.

Johnson, Dr. Anita: A nutritionist on the expedition to Arctic Canada with whom Humbert and several other men engaged in sexual activities. She was sent home early during the expedition.

Junks, The: Neighbors of the Hazes in Ramsdale.

Kenny: He delivers the paper in the Hazes neighborhood in Ramsdale.

Kilmerite: In reference to Joyce Kilmer, New Jersey poet (born 1886). His fame rests entirely on his 12-line poem entitled "Trees", which contains the almost proverbial line: "I think I shall never see / A poem as lovely as a tree." The previous, published in the 1913 issue of *Poetry*, however, was not his best work, and its mixed metaphors came to serve as a negative example for the New Critics. Kilmer's best poetry discusses the topic of war. Ironically, he was killed off the field of battle in France on July 30, 1918.

The Kreutzer Sonata: (1898) A painting by Rene Prinet of a violinist and pianist who have probably just finished playing Beethoven's "Kreutzer Sonata"; composed in 1805 and dedicated to Rodolphe Kreutzer. Also a story by Leo Tolstoy.

Lacour, Mme.: A woman murdered by a lover in Alres, southern France, while her husband watched. The assailant was saved from capture by a bomb blast in an adjacent building which caused a commotion large enough to allow the murderer to escape.

Lake Climax: The large and "populous" lake near Camp Q out of which

Charlie would fish contraceptives for his trysts with Barbara Burke, Phyllis Chatfield, and Dolores each morning. It is supposedly named for a booming industrial town nearby.

Lambert Lambert: One of several pseudonyms Humbert thinks about for his *Confessions of a White Widowed Male* before chosing Humbert Humbert. (See also Mesmer Mesmer and Otto Otto.)

Laodicean: In this context, it means indifferent or lukewarm, usually as it pertains to religion, although here "non-Laodicean" describes the tendency for showers to turn unpredictably hot or cold.

Lasalle, Frank: A fifty-year-old mechanic accused of molesting eleven-year-old Sally Horner in 1948.

Laura: Petrarch's lost love.

Leigh, Annabel: A girl of English and Dutch ancestry whose name refers to Edgar Allan Poe's poem "Annabel Lee." She and Humbert had met at the beach one summer in their early adolescence, and it was to their thwarted attempts at making love Humbert attributes his lust for nymphets.

Leigh, Mr. and Mrs.: Annabel's parents.

Lepchas: A Mongoloid people of India with a rather flexible view of inter-generational copulation.

Lepingville: A town near where Charlotte Haze is supposedly hospitalized for abominable abdominal pains. Also a town where a great poet resided in the early nineteenth century and where Humbert tells Lolita they will take in all the shows. In fact, it is in a gas station near there that he reveals her mother is dead, and proceeds to placate her with gifts he buys in the town.

Lester, Miss: A "tweedy and short-haired" neighbor of Humbert's on Thayer St. in Beardsley, and a professor of English at Beardsley College.

Lilith: In Jewish legends, Adam's wife before Eve.

Little Carmen: Lolita's favorite record; Humbert calls it "Dwarf Conductors."

The Little Nymph: (1940) Clare Quilty's most successful play; it traveled 14,000 miles and was played 280 times.

Litam, Ned: The man in California who taught Lolita a tennis volley which Humbert likes to watch.

Lolita (character): Also, Lo, Lola, Dolly, and Dolores Haze. She is the central object of Humbert's lust, love, admiration, and obsession. Shortly after first seeing her on the piazza, Humbert makes her his solipsistic ideal; she becomes his archetypal nymphet and eclipses the influence and memory of the past 25 years of his life.

Lorrain, Claude: Claude Lorrain is often said to be the father of the European tradition of landscape painting. Born in France in 1600, Lorrain is usually considered an Italian painter, as he lived in that country for most of his life. Known also as a master of painting the beauty and variety of natural light, Lorrain exercised an influence on the landscape painters of the 19th century as well as the French impressionists. He died in Rome in 1682 at the age of 82.

Lourdes, Grotto of: The town of Lourdes is located in southwestern France. In 1858, fourteen year old Bernadette Soubirous (now a saint) was said to have numerous religious visions at a grotto located there. In 1876 a basilica was built at the Grotto of Lourdes, which has become a popular tourist destination, in part from the miraculous healing power which is said to originate from the spot of Bernadette's visions. An underground church was completed near the shrine in 1958. The whereabouts of a replica in Louisiana is variously given by the readers of the web version of this document as New Iberia and St. Martinsville. The editor has not been able to confirm either of these theories.

Lyon: A city in France. Humbert attends high school there.

Madeleine: Church of Magdalene in Paris. Humbert meets a streetwalker there.

Magdelein: German for a little girl or lassie. Humbert speaks of making a "clean" home for Lolita and finding himself a Magdelein among Lolita's friends (as opposed to Lolita).

Magnolia Garden: Best guesses locate Magnolia Garden in the Magnolia Plantation in Charleston, South Carolina.

Main Street: Street in Wace where Humbert searches for his temporarily lost Lolita.

Mann Act: Otherwise known as the White Slave Traffic Act, the Mann Act (authored by Illinois Republican Representative James Mann and passed by Congress in 1910), prohibited the interstate transportation of women for immoral purposes. Prostitution in the United States was unregulated until the Mann act was passed. By 1915, nearly all of the states, with the exception of what was then the "frontier," had banned the existence of brothels. Today, one found in violation of the Mann Act can be fined $5,000, or imprisoned for 5 years, or both. If a minor is involved, the penalty might be doubled.

Marat, Jean-Paul: (1743-1793) French revolutionary stabbed while bathing.

May 30: A Fast Day in New Hampshire but not in the Carolinas.

McCoo, Mr.: An impoverished cousin of one of Humbert's uncle's old employees. He is retired and has a wife and two girls (one is twelve). Humbert originally went to Ramsdale with the intention of rooming with the McCoos, but their house burned before his arrival.

McCoo, Virginia: Also Ginny. The twelve year old daughter of Mr. McCoo; Humbert was motivated to move to Ramsdale by the prospect of living in the same house with this prospective nymphet. She is no nymphet. She suffered from polio as a child and probably is deformed or handicapped. Lolita describes her as mean and a lame fright.

McFate's secretary: Continuously responsible for interupting Humbert's idyllic plans. This inept secretary acts as a "secondary fate."

Menninger Foundation, The: The Menninger Clinic for psychiatry was founded by Charles Menninger in Topeka, Kansas in 1920, and is considered the first attempt to gather many specialists in one centralized facility. The Menninger Foundation was formed in 1941 in order to educate professionals and conduct psychiatric research.

Mesmer Mesmer: One of several pseudonyms Humbert thinks about before choosing Humbert Humbert. (See also Otto Otto and Lambert Lambert.)

Milner Pass: Part of Rocky Mountain National Park near Estes Park, Colorado. Milner Pass (elevation 10,759 feet) marks the spot where the Continental Divide crosses the Trail Ridge Road.

Mirana Motel: One of the many motels in which Humbert and Lolita spend the night. The motel shares its name with the Hotel Mirana where Humbert first met his Annabell Leigh.

Molnar, Dr.: Beardsly dentist who removes most of Humbert's teeth and replaces them with dentures.

Monique: A childlike prostitute Humbert meets in Paris.

A Murder Is Announced: The title of a novel by the English mystery writer Agatha Christie (pub. 1950).

My Cue: Vivian Darkbloom's biographical book on Clare Quilty.

Negro: Ms. Opposite's cheerful chauffeur who drives Humbert to 342 Lawn Street.

Nansen: A travel document for emigres.

Nefertiti, Queen: See King Ahnaten.

New York, NY: Humbert moved to New York in 1940 to write perfume ads for his uncle's company; here he also worked 15 hours a day on his comparative history of French Literature for English-speaking students.

Nurse Lore: See Lore, Mary.

Nymphet: "Between the age limits of nine and fourteen there occur maidens who, to certain bewitched travelers, twice or many times older than they, reveal their true nature which is not human, but nymphic (that is, demoniac); and these chosen creatures I propose to designate as 'nymphets.'" They do not occur in polar regions.

Opal: One of Lolita's companions at the Beardsley School for Women: a "bashful, formless, bespectacled, bepimpled creature" whom Lolita bullies.

Opposite, Miss: An elderly, wheelchair-bound lady who lives across the street from 342 Lawn Street in Ramsdale.

Otto Otto: One of several pseudonyms Humbert thinks about before chosing Humbert Humbert. (See also Mesmer Mesmer and Lambert Lambert.)

Our Glass Lake: Also Hour Glass Lake, a lake near Ramsdale that Humbert wants to visit with Lo. It becomes an emblem of his hope for fulfilling his desire, and the trips are continually canceled by Mrs. Haze or bad weather.

Papa's Purple Pills: Humbert believes them to be sleeping pills, telling Lolita they are made of summer skies, plums and figs and the grape-blood of emperors. He proceeds to tell Lo that they are really Vitamin X, to make one strong as an ox or an ax. These pills did not belong to the barbiturate family as Humbert had believed, but were merely a mild sedative.

Park, The: Humbert and Lolita get lost in the park before finding The Enchanted Hunters. The dark park was as black as the sins it concealed.

Parkington: Town where Humbert spends the night before retrieving Lolita from Camp Q 100 miles away. He had intended to leave the town at 9:30 but did not actually depart until near noon because of a dead battery.

Pavor Manor: Clare Quilty's ancestral home on Grimm Road, near Parkington.

Phalen, Miss: The caretaker of the farmhouse in Appalachia where Dolores had spent a dreary summer. It is this house that Humbert threatens to send Dolores to force her into compliance.

Pierre Point, Melville Sound: An imaginary place derived from the once controversial novel *Pierre* (1852) by Herman Melville (1819-1891).

Pichon: Author of *La Beauté Humaine*.

Pilvon and Zapel: The authors of "an impressive volume on the legal side of marriage." They neglect quite naturally—to discuss the situation of "stepfathers with motherless girls on their hands and knees."

Pinedale: A city in southwestern Wyoming, located approximately 60 miles from Farson.

Pinski, Milton: A schoolboy contemporary of Dolores Haze and Eva Rosen, whose talking about music Eva ranks as worse than death.

Portugal: Humbert spent the winter of 1939-40 here before coming to America.

Potts, Dr.: Worker at The Enchanted Hunters. Pink and bald with white hairs growing out of his orifices.

Priap: Greco-Roman god of fertility and procreation; son of Dionysus and Aphrodite.

Pym, Roland: (b.1922) Name derived from Edgar Allan Poe's *The Narrative of A. Gordon Pym.* An actor whose name is on the coincidental page in *Who's Who in the Limelight* and has appeared in "Two Blocks from Here," "The Girl in Green," "Scrambled Husbands," "The Strange Mushroom," "Touch and Go," "John Lovely" and "I was Dreaming of You."

Quilty, Clare: (b. 1911) American playwright, author of *The Little Nymph, The Lady Who Loved Lightning, Dark Age, The Strange Mushroom, Fatherly Love,* and others (such as the screenplay *Golden Guts*). Murdered by Humbert. Hobbies are fast cars, photography, pornography, and pets. Writer in Dromes ad. Also co-author of the play *Children-Colors*. He is responsible for making good Dolores Haze's escape at Elphinstone. He takes Lo to Duk Duk Ranch, where he apparently likes to film his friends engaging in all manners of sexual debauchery.

Quilty, Ivor: A fat Ramsdale dentist; uncle of Clare Quilty. In order to find out where Clare can be found, Humbert visits Dr. Quilty under the pretense of having his remaining teeth pulled and replaced by dentures.

Quine, Dolores: (b. 1882) Name listed below Clare Quilty in *Who's Who . . .* that Humbert associates with Dolores Haze. An actress who debuted in 1904 in *Never Talk to Strangers* and "disappeared" later in many other plays as H.H. spoonerizes concepts.

Rahab: In Joshua 2:-1-21 she is the Canaanite prostitute.

Ramsdale: A generic New England town with elms and a white church. Humbert moves to Ramsdale in 1947 and there comes into contact with Lolita.

Ramsdale Journal: Local newspaper for Ramsdale. Also where Humbert placed his and Charlotte's wedding announcement.

Ray, John Jr., Ph.D.: The author of the Foreword to *Lolita.*

Red: See Bill Mead.

'Red Sweater': Humbert's mental designation for a boy who happens to walk Lolita home one day from the Beardsley School for Girls.

Review of Anthropology: A magazine in which Humbert looks for the results from the study in which Valeria and Maximovich participated.

Rita: Humbert's hard drinking adult female companion. Married a Florida hotel owner.

Ronsard: See de Ronsard, Pierre.

Rose: See Hamilton, Mary Rose.

Rosen, Eva: A "displaced little person from France" and companion of Lolita's at the Beardsley School for Girls. Humbert describes her as a nymphet, but Lolita stops associating with her before Humbert gets to know her well (possibly to prevent any amorous intentions on Humbert's part).

Russian Gultch State Park: Located along the Russian River in Mendocino County, California.

Sade's *Justine*: Justine is a persecuted heroine in the work by that title, written by the Marquis de Sade, a notorious French writer whose works are often considered blasphemous and pornographic. Clare Quilty is implicitly compared to de Sade on page 276.

Saguaro: A large cactus which is found in northern Mexico.

Schiller, Paul: A man in Coalmont working in a furniture business; Richard Schiller is the son of a cousin of his.

Schiller, Richard F.: a.k.a. Dick Skiller (Dick's Killer). The husband of seventeen year old Dolores Haze. His hearing was damaged in Italy (presumably) during World War II. All indications show that he and Dolores went to Alaska where Dick had gotten a job in his highly-specialized mechanical field; they were to live with Dick's brother. Dick has a bad complexion and fine hands.

Schiller, Mrs. Richard F.: Died in childbirth giving birth to a stillborn girl, on Christmas Day 1952. She is in actuality Dolores Haze, known by her married name.

Schwarzmann, Dr. Blanche: (Dr. Whitewoman Blackman) Speculates that at least 12% of American adult males share Humbert's predilections.

Scotty's Castle: Built by Walter Scott (also known as Death Valley Scotty) in the late 1920s in Death Valley, California. Scotty moved to Death Valley in search of gold in the late 1890s. He claimed to be unsuccessful in his search, yet he is notorious for his wild spending sprees. It remains a mystery how Scotty procured the funds to build his castle. Today the site is one of Death Valley's most popular tourist attractions.

Sicilians: Inhabitants of Sicily. In an attempt to legitimize their relationship, Humbert tries to convince Dolores that among the Sicilians it is regular practice for fathers and daughters to participate in incest.

Silver Spur Court: Humbert orders a two-room cabin at Silver Spur Court in Elphinstone. The cabin reminds Humbert of their first journey, and he reflects on how different things are now.

Snow, Colorado: Humbert takes Lolita to a Colorado resort between Snow and Elphinstone.

Stevenson, R.L.: Scottish novelist, poet, travel writer, and essayist, born in Edinburgh in 1850. He is most famous for his three classics: *Treasure*

Island, Kidnapped, and *Doctor Jekyll and Mr. Hyde.* Said to be one of the best British writers of the late 19th century, Stevenson gained notoriety in England as an essayist. In 1876, Stevenson met an estranged American woman named Fanny Osborne, and his devotion to her led him to travel to San Francisco in 1879. He moved with his wife to Samoa in 1890, where he eventually died in 1894. Nabokov taught *Doctor Jekyll and Mr. Hyde* at Cornell University.

Swine, Mr.: Desk clerk at The Enchanted Hunters; Humbert mistakenly refers to him as Mr. Swoon.

Swoons: The family at The Enchanted Hunters that received the spare cot that was in room 49.

Sybil: Humbert's so-so prophetic aunt.

Talbot, Elizabeth: The "little lesbian" whom Humbert suspects (correctly) of having taught Dolores "various manipulations" during previous years' summer camp. He remembers with irony that Charlotte had often referred to her daughter's knowing the "Talbot girl."

Taxovich, Mr.: Also Maximovich. The man for whom Valeria leaves Humbert and with whom she moves to California.

Tennis: See Wills, Helen.

Tony: A florid-faced fellow with blue eyes who is one of a group of people that come to Clare Quilty's house as Humbert is murdering him. They interpret the shooting and Clare's struggle for life as a staged event for their pleasure.

Trapp, Gustave: a.k.a. Detective Trapp. The name Humbert assigns to the driver of the Aztec Red Convertible. At first, Trapp drives the red convertible, but pursuant cars are usually blue and of "the Chevrolet genus." Humbert attributes the name Trapp to his pursuer because the driver looks like Gustave Trapp, a deceased cousin of Humbert's father. He is remembered particularly for the use of the expression, "sicher ist sicher."

Uncle Tom: The hunched back and hoary black porter at The Enchanted Hunters.

A Vagabond in Italy: A novel by Percy Elphinstone in the library of a prison where Humbert is awaiting trial.

Valeria: Humbert's nubile first wife who turns overnight into a "puffy, short-legged, big-breasted and practically brainless baba." Died in childbirth around 1945.

van Ness, Vanessa: Mrs. Leigh's maiden name.

Vaucluse: An area of Southeastern France, often given as home to Petrarch.

Venice Revisited: Another novel in the prison library written by Percy Elphinstone (pub. 1868).

Vibrissa: Clare Quilty's char woman who has three breasts. Clare Quilty offers her to Humbert if Humbert will spare Quilty's life.

Virgil: (70-19 BC) A Latin poet whom Humbert sees as homosexual.

Virginia: (1823-1847) Virginia Clemm, wife and cousin of Edgar Allan Poe whom he married when she was 13 years old.

Walton Inn: A restaurant in Beardsley which Humbert describes as tacky and unsanitary.

Wace: The town where Humbert loses Lolita for a brief period of time. When she returns she claims to have run into an old classmate and lost track of time.

Weiss, Melanie: Explorer and psychoanalyst who compiled the folio *Bagration Island*, containing over 800 pictures of penises she examined and measured in 1932 on Bagration, in the Barda Sea.

West, Mr.: Humbert's designation for his west-door neighbor on Thayer St. in Beardsley, with whom he has no contact.

Who's Who in the Limelight: An entertainment magazine that contains "actors, producers, playwrights, and shots of static scenes." In the 1946 edition Humbert finds the page which he refers to as a coincidence that "poets love."

Widworth, Mass.: There on August 5, 1955, the supercilious John Ray, Jr. pens the foreword to *Lolita*.

Wills, Helen: The top female tennis player in the world for eight years (1927-33 and 1935). Her book *Tennis* is one of the books Humbert travels sixty miles to get for Lolita. Interestingly, Humbert mentions only that Wills had won the National Junior Girls Singles at age fifteen.

Wimbeldon: Humbert imagines that Lolita would have been a tennis star, competing in the Wimbeldon tournament were it not for him.

'Windbreaker': Humbert's mental designation for a boy who happens to speak to Lolita outside a restaurant in Beardsley.

Windmuller, Louise: Daughter of Mr. Windmuller.

Windmuller, Mr.: A resident of Ramsdale who desires to have his identity suppressed by John Ray, Jr. He was responsible for Humbert's financial concerns in Ramsdale.

Woolsey, John M.: The Supreme Court justice who cleared James Joyce's *Ulysses* of obscenity charges.

Zemfirian: An obscure language. See Basque.

Numbered Entries

10 **Killer Street:** "A tenement house' in Coalmont where Richard Schiller once resided with his wife Dolores.

14 **Thayer Street:** The residence of Humbert's friend at the Beardsley College for Women, Gaston Godin; Humbert moves onto Thayer St. when he arrives in Beardsley.

"342": The room number Humbert and Lolita stay in at The Enchanted Hunters. A double-bed room full of mirrors and furniture pieces in twos (bedtables, chairs, nightlamps); the number of "hotels, motels and tourist homes" Humbert registered in while pursuing Lolita.

342 **Lawn Street:** The residence of Lolita and Mrs. Haze in Ramsdale. ✧

April Bernard

April Bernard is the author of three poetry collections: *Swan Electric, Psalms,* and *Blackbird Bye Bye,* and one novel, *Pirate Jenny.* Her work has appeared in *The New Yorker, The Boston Review, Agni, Ploughshares, Parnassus,* and *The New York Review of Books* and is included in *The Penguin Book of the Sonnet: 500 Years of a Classic Tradition in English* and *By Herself: Women Reclaim Poetry.* She is also the recipient of a Guggenheim Award. Ms. Bernard lives in Bennington, VT, where she teaches at Bennington College. The following interview took place in the fall of 2001.

REB LIVINGSTON: In your new book, *Swan Electric,* your poetry seems to take a turn from your last book, *Psalms,* to being more narrative and accessible, perhaps even borderline confessional. Was that a conscious decision or did it just happen?

APRIL BERNARD: I have always struggled with both of those issues, clarity and the use of personal material, in my work. Of course *I* find *Psalms* utterly lucid, and so I'm always confused when other people find any of it confusing. I think the poems in *Psalms* are infinitely more personal than anything else I've ever done—my design was for it to be a public voice, the voice of a psalmist, speaking on private matters. I was trying to write something in the spirit of David and the other psalmists of the Old Testament. Using the personal lament, the personal praise, and the personal experience to speak for the congregation, the group. It was meant to be both personal and public at the same time.

None of those self-conscious considerations animate the new poems in *Swan Electric* at all. They were much more viscerally generated, and at the same time I also deliberately worked to be understood. I had the experience for several years after *Psalms* came out, hearing again and again from people that had been puzzled. Not even my students or friends got the stuff that I thought of as excruciatingly self-revelatory. Maybe the new poems seem more personal simply because they're clearer.

I take everything personally, which I think most writers do. I take the troubles of the world personally. I tend to write them through a filter of the personal even when I'm trying to address something much bigger than myself, which I hope is most of the time.

Q: One theme that you continue with in *Swan Electric* is urban living. There's grit, but also a bit of sadness. Are these urban sadnesses or human sadnesses?

A: They're human sadness. I think you're referring mostly to the memoir sequence, which covers my life in the 1980s, when I was living in the East Village in New York. Those poems are very urban, but they're about the sadness and idiocy of being young. They're about the sadness of a first love and first hope and the excitement of feeling like you and your friends rule the world and then learning that you don't. I don't mean "ruling the world" in any sort of maniacal way, but as artists. There was a group of us making movies and writing books and playing music in clubs. We thought we were It.

Q: How long has it been since you've lived in New York City?

A: My husband and I left the city in 1997. We were going to have a baby, and we wanted to live where there would be room to keep him someplace besides the bathtub.

Q: Did the September 11 tragedy affect the way you look at your New York poems?

A: Yes, it does, actually, although of course I wrote them earlier. I'd be really curious to see if *you* read them in that light. I have missed New York just passionately since September 11. I want to move back there. I want to go home. I feel the ruefulness in my own poems keenly, and I kind of want to stop that ruefulness and be ambitious and idealistic again and help save the city.

Q: I was struck by the thought of Sept.11, when reading one poem in particular, "She Runs With Her Skirts Up." It reads almost as an eerie prophecy.

A: Really?

Q: It kind of freaked me out, not that it was about it, but some of the imagery.

A: It's about having a kid, which I'm sure you guessed . . .

Q: Yes, but it starts off with the line "All those stories come tumbling" and goes on:

> over the chopped sea waves and the broken stones of the road,
> they come tumbling and running like puppies, or children,
> something like that, since surely no crowd of men in fedoras

ever laughed and nickered as they ran and fell,
racing, out of breath, to tell us.

Hey to the red mitten, no, not stained with blood,
that's berry juice from a hawthorne tree in a holiday mood –
and Hey to the hand that tucks the golden curls
back under the cap and wishes him a bonny speedy journey.

When the wind's from the north, the story goes,
the whisky sting reds the nose and warms the bones.
She runs with her skirts up, in woolen stockings,
and the bundle on the sleigh flickers like blinking
in the clatter of the film through sprockets,
because it's all happening, again, in broad day this time.

A: Well, that's interesting, and scary. But for me it's all about having a kid.
The image of film flickering through sprockets is home movies of me as a
child versus the reality of being a mom. So instead of seeing it as dim and
the clattering with the odd colors of a home movie memory, I'm pulling
my own son in a sled, in daylight, in the snow.

Q: Do you have an opinion about the quick proliferation of poems and
essays that deal with the tragedy?

A: I think it's inevitable. But of course that incredible poem by Adam
Zagajewski, "Try to Praise the Mutilated World," on the back page of *The
New Yorker*, had been written before the tragedy—not as direct editorial
comment.
  As for the ones that do get written about September 11—I suppose
there may be the rare poet who, as W.H. Auden was, can be a chronicler
and elegist for current events. But that's all New Yorkers do, is tell each
other stories of where they were and what they saw. It appears to be an
essential part of that kind of trauma.

Q: What influence, if any, does motherhood have on your work?

A: "She Runs with Her Skirts Up" is the only poem I've written about
being a mother, except (tangentially) one called "Fort-Da," which is a nasty
poem. So motherhood hasn't affected my subject matter. Maybe it's
because I had my son when I was older. I was already me, very much me.
He's changed my life, but motherhood hasn't changed my work in ways
that I've seen. It's made writing harder because of time. But I don't know.
Someone else will have to tell me if it's changed my work because I don't
see it. I certainly don't feel the impulse to write about him; I feel too
protective of him to do that.

Q: Have you written any birth poems?

A: No, no, noooo (laughs). But I don't write that way about myself anyway.

Q: The first section of *Swan Electric* is almost all sonnets, and some of your poems have been anthologized in *The Penguin Book of the Sonnet: 500 Years of a Classic Tradition in English*, edited by Phillis Levin. What is it about the form that attracts you?

A: I'm obsessed with sonnets. When the first English sonneteers translated from the Italian, they developed a new structure for the sonnet, which was not the meditative, circular structure of the Italian, but something else: an argument. Going stanza by stanza, the English sonnet argues: This; and this; BUT this; and moreover. That argument structure of the sonnet seems to me so useful, so interesting; it dictates a motion for the poem.

I'm not particularly excited about iambic pentameter per se. I'm classically enough trained that I think it's very important to know what iambic pentameter is and to be able to write it (and other meters) and to be able to write plausible rhymed verse—although end-rhymes in English poetry are almost inevitably clunky. In the sonnet, it's the structure of the argument that I find so wonderful, how form can shape the way you think, and if you think in sonnets long enough, every subject becomes a containable four-part "This; and this; BUT this; and moreover." Historically, sonnets are useful for talking someone into bed, for getting revenge, for explaining why things are the way they are even though you don't like it, for explaining why things are the way they are and how you will change them.

When people today write any old fourteen-line poem and call it a sonnet, they miss the essence of the sonnet. I think that looseness is also rather charming—they can call them anything they want—but for me the essential part of a sonnet in English is this argument structure. Especially because I find myself using the sonnet as a way of arguing myself out of a personal cul-de-sac. When I'm stuck at a bad place emotionally, I can use a sonnet to explore, as it were, the stanza-room I'm in. I can use the sonnet as a way of covering the bases—the going to the corners of the room and finally in the fourth corner, opening the door to go out. It's self-argument as a meditation.

Q: You tend to blend traditional forms with free verse. When reading your poetry, sometimes I get a very classical sensibility and other times very contemporary. It's almost as if your poems time travel. Is that a technique you intentionally apply?

A: I think I'm just a magpie. My use of the sonnet form is very intentional but the other stuff, I don't know. I teach versification and I'm trained in it. I can write quatrains and ballads and all, but they just sound terrible. There's no other strict form besides the sonnet that I really use. I tend to allow my poems to generate their own form. Once it's on the page I start to see a shape to it and I say organically this wants to be a poem in triplets or this wants to be a poem with really long lines. As I'm revising it I allow it to be the thing it seems to want to be. But it pretty much has to be generated from within. I would say that it's not very conscious, it's really much more an intuitive thing. Although I do actually write formal poems as exercises when I'm stuck.

Q: Do those ever turn out?

A: Never (laughs). But they're still good to do. Sometimes they turn out as jokes that I give to friends. I write a fair number of Emily Dickinson imitations as letters or communications with friends. Once you master the gross aspects of her style and meter, it's a very funny way to talk to someone else. I find her hilarious.

Q: Do you believe that a reader has to labor and earn the fruits of a poem?

A: Recently I've been trying to explain to students why poems are sometimes so difficult and about the aesthetic of difficulty. My best explanation involves the premise that a poem is capturing a moment of absolute intense emotion. In the throes of an intense emotion, you can't possibly write; your back is flat on the floor. So by the time you get to writing the poem, you're trying to capture that emotion and put it in a usable form. I think the difficult, elaborated aspects of a poem are like the wrapping on a present. It becomes a means of conveyance to hand the poem to somebody else because you can't just hurl the emotion at them. You have to give it to them in a form that is stable and that won't explode. It's like putting dynamite in a nice box and then you hand the box, which is the poem, to the other person and the other person has to unpack it. If you're lucky, they will enjoy the unwrapping. Part of the purposeful difficulty of the poem is meant to prolong the unwrapping process and to prolong the expectation.

But I wouldn't think of it as earning the enjoyment, because I don't like to think of a poem as labor. The difficulty must be part of the pleasure. And once the reader has unwrapped it and found that dynamite, that center thing, then, if you're lucky and your poem does the right job, then your reader falls over backwards. But if you'd just thrown it at him or handed it to him in a raw form, that wouldn't have worked.

Q: You've written about both Anne Sexton and Sylvia Plath. How influenced were you by their work?

A: I remember feeling very sorry for Anne Sexton when I first read her. I couldn't have been older than 14 or 15. "How interesting and horrifying, that is what it might mean to be a grown-up woman," I remember thinking, "Oh dear, this is very bad news." Bad news about sex, bad news about how you feel about yourself. I don't know if I thought those were great poems or not. I don't think I did.

Plath, from the minute I read her, I thought she was great. I didn't think it was bad news at all. In fact, I couldn't reconcile the knowledge that she killed herself with the poems because the poems seemed to be so alive. I thought she was the most vibrant, wonderful person in the world, why would she kill herself? They didn't go together. I've never seen them as symptomatic of illness. That's the thing about art; it's bigger and better than we are. The "we" who make it.

In terms of Plath's influence, I think it was more of a permission thing. Permission to be tough on the page. Permission to be elusive, to be difficult. Permission to be angry.

Q: Do you think that Plath and Sexton have the same influence on emerging 20-something female poets today as they did on female poets from your generation?

A: I don't think Sexton does at all. I think Sexton has faded, as I think the quality of work would make happen anyway.

Plath still seems to be a pretty big influence on people. Certainly undergraduates know who she is and know something about her work—usually the wrong things. But I don't think the young women that I encounter in college these days need the same kind of permission to write that I did when I was younger. What they do need permission for and encouragement about is to take themselves seriously, but that's another question.

Q: I think saying that you're a poet has many negative connotations. If you meet someone at a non-literary party and say that you're a poet, people look at you like you're a freak. Usually poets in public say that they're "writers" or "teachers." Just about anything sounds better than poet.

A: Right. But the young men that I teach at a college level, those among them who write poetry, are very ambitious. They're ambitious for the work. They may know that it's a hopeless business to be a poet in our culture and in our civilization. But they're very ambitious for the poems.

The young women are more likely to be writing to please themselves or to make something pretty or to express themselves in a very soft way.

The young men want to read the big names and get on the stage with them. They want to know famous poets, and they're ambitious in a worldly way. Not that the world of poets is that exciting (laughs).

Q: What poet of your generation do you most admire?

A: A couple. In the immediate older generation, I'm crazy about Frank Bidart. I love W.S. Merwin and John Ashbery. Those three poets are pretty important to me. There's a lot about Jorie Graham's work that I admire and love. I'm fascinated by the chilly heartbreak of her work. Of my peers, there are a few poets practically my exact age that I think are just great. They are Henri Cole, Lucie Brock-Broido, and Wayne Koestenbaum.

Q: Why them?

A: They're not similar exactly. What we all have in common has to do with a level of linguistic hysteria—a passionate attachment to language on a sensual level at the expense of everything else. It's making a choice that has to do with sound and beauty and the taste of the words.

The issues that each of us writes about are very different, but we all have that kind of foolish devotion to sounds and a kind of baroqueness, a real baroque quality as in a baroque pearl, as something natural that got twisted towards the extreme. I mean something decorated but very raw at the same time. In fact, I think one way of describing the English language itself would be to say it's very decorated and very raw at the same time.

Q: But you're not talking about what we would call *language* poetry, are you?

A: No, but *language* poets are an interesting phenomenon, though I think their moment has passed. I remain unconvinced that language is a good place to do abstract work. That kind of abstract work. I think the analogy that is most frequently drawn for *language* poetry is the analogy with abstract painting. I love abstract painting. But the visual field can hold your interest with pattern, balance, and color in a way that the visual field on a page for a poem just doesn't because we have to read linearly (it's how our brains organize language), so we're trapped in linearity. Consequently, the same things that can give us pleasure in an abstract painting do not give us pleasure on the page. That's where I think the analogy between abstract painting and abstract poetry breaks down.

I also fundamentally disagree with the very heartfelt and serious views from Charles Bernstein and others, that the English language has been so corrupted by commercialism that you can't hope to say anything uncorrupted in it. I don't think the English language has been ruined by commercialism. I think commercialism is a terrible problem, but I don't think it has altered the way we can hear and see language when it's used well. I think that the fight is worth fighting, and I don't feel like ceding English as a narrative and linear language to the world of commerce. I don't think that commerce owns it, and if it's trying to, I want to fight for it. I want to fight on the same turf, because I love the language I was lucky enough to be born into.

Q: What poet do you believe is most unfairly overlooked?

A: Oh, Charlotte Mew. She's not completely overlooked, though—there's probably a Charlotte Mew Revival as we speak (laughs). I'm having my own personal revival of Dryden. I love Dryden these days.

I just reread the "Song for St. Cecilia's Day" and thought it was the most beautiful poem I've read in my life. It isn't, but it felt like it when I was reading it. I don't think Dryden is overlooked, just not fashionable.

Q: To whom do you show your work for first readings and criticism?

A: Sometimes Wayne Koestenbaum and I exchange work. Most recently in the last few years, I have shown my work to my friend Alice Mattison, the writer. She's a really good first critic for me.

Q: Are you sending work out to readers for the criticism or affirmation or something else?

A: That's a very good question. I used to read my stuff to John Ash, who is a wonderful reader and poet. He now lives in Turkey, and we're not in touch as much as we used to be. John was great because he was really rude sometimes, and he would say, "That's terrible," or "I don't get it at all," or "Where's the second half of the poem?" But because I adored him and trusted him completely and loved his work (and could be just as rude to him), it was very useful.

Most people I'm too touchy to hear that from. But Alice is very good about telling me where she's confused. It is one of the best things another reader can do for you. Those kinds of notes along the side of the page: "I got lost here."

But it's ridiculous that I'm a teacher because mostly I can't bear to be criticized. On the other hand, I'm very tough on my own work. Once I've decided that it's sort of ok, it takes a lot to shake me from that.

Q: You've taught at Barnard, Yale, Amherst College, and Columbia University, and now you are at Bennington College, both in undergraduate literature and the low-residency MFA program. Besides a paycheck, what, if anything, do you get out of being a teacher of literature and writing?

A: (laughs) I love teaching. First of all, the paycheck is very important. But

I think that even if I lived in a fantastic world where I had all the money I wanted, I would still teach. I don't think I would teach as much. But I would teach literature. Not writing, probably, but definitely literature. I love teaching literature because every time you have to stand up and talk you learn something new. It's an absolutely selfish way of pursuing my own education. And at the same time, I also believe I am doing something useful in the world—specifically, for my students—in passing on my passionate belief in the power and the glory of literature. What I get out of teaching writing is that, once in a while, the miraculous happens, and I get excited by students' work so that I'm feeding off them as much as they're feeding off me.

Q: Do you have any preference between teaching undergraduate and graduate writing?

A: Undergraduates, in some ways, are a lot more fun. You can surprise and astonish them, like you just invented the wheel and they've watched you do it and they think you're a genius. Wooo, it goes around and around! My Bennington College students are also so independent and funny and generous. Graduate students are more like colleagues, so you can have real conversations. When graduate students are not overly defensive about the business of being a student, they're great.

Q: You have a BA in literature from Harvard. Did you study with Elizabeth Bishop while you were there?

A: I did. It's not a horrible exaggeration to say that one of the main reasons I went to Harvard was because she was listed in the catalog as one of their professors. I really loved Elizabeth Bishop's work before most people I knew had ever heard of her. "The Fish" was anthologized in a high school text, which was where I first read her when I was 13. I felt that the world had changed. I thought that poem was so great, but I also thought it was speaking specifically to me, giving me a piece of information. That piece of information, what I needed to hear was, "You can do anything." That poem leaps right off the page into the ether at the end. I thought: "Oh, I guess you can do anything in a poem." It was a whole new piece of permission.

Maybe it also was that Bishop's language wasn't "poetical." It must have been one of the first times I connected with a poem that had been written by a 20th-century poet. For Bishop, it has to do with understatement. In one of her letters from Brazil, she once complained that the problem with Portuguese is that the language has no word for understatement. Which itself is the understatement of all time about her.

When I got to Harvard, I was too intimidated; I didn't even apply to be in her class. I didn't know you could. I was one of those dopey undergraduates who never really knew what was going on. Then in my junior year I took her literature seminar, sort of "My Favorite Poets by Elizabeth Bishop." We read Robert Frost, Wallace Stevens, Marianne Moore, and Robert Lowell. She was such a dreary teacher and such a snappy person. She was not very approachable, but another student and I were brazen and we invited ourselves over to her house for tea, and I had tea with her a few times after that. She never wanted to talk about poetry. She was friendly and chatty and wanted to know all about my family and wanted to talk about her travels. She was doing that "impression of an ordinary woman" that James Merrill has referred to.

She was incredibly important to me even though the class was almost useless. Except that she had us write an imitation of Marianne Moore. She said that in my poem, I caught her tone exactly, but that it wasn't nearly beautiful enough. It was wonderful to be praised and insulted in the same sentence. I think she got interested in me as a person because she noticed I had a good mimic's ear. I still have that poem somewhere in my files. It's about a gecko.

Q: I've read stories that she made impossibly high demands on her students. Was that your impression?

A: No. Maybe she was in her writing classes, but I didn't take her writing classes. My memory of her was someone who hated being in the classroom and couldn't wait to get out. She didn't really like people to be stupid, so she wasn't very pleasant to people who asked her stupid questions.

Q: What did you study while you were a graduate student at Yale?

A: I went to Yale to get my PhD in English Literature. The first and only year I was there I did the basic class work. I did have one wonderful class, which was Harold Bloom's seminar on Freud. It was like watching Jacob wrestle with the angel. I don't think that Bloom would deny the obvious, which is that his relationship to Freud embodies his own theory of the threatening immediate precursor. Bloom clearly feels this attachment and rivalry with Freud that makes his readings of Freud's works fascinating. It was an absolutely riveting experience. He also made me see how funny Freud was, which I hadn't really realized.

Q: Was the PhD program just not your cup of tea? Why did you leave?

A: Oh it definitely wasn't my cup of tea. At the time the Yale literature program was pretty tough; it was kind of a split between the old-guard, old-fashioned English literature types and the Paul de Man post structuralist people.

Q: That had to be in the thick of it then.

A: Yes, but it wasn't that I was opposed to any particular aspect of the training being offered there. I just found myself unable to write poems, and I don't know if that's because I was such a sensitive plant or because there was, as I imagined at the time, an attitude at Yale of loathing the writer. There may or may not have been; it could have been all my projection. Whether you were old school or new school, in terms of a critical approach to literature, there was this sense that the writer was a slob, a useless slob who had accidentally generated this thing, this poem or novel that we are bound to study. But "we," the academics and critics, are so much smarter and more interesting than the slob who generated this work. I was depressed by this attitude.

Q: You found this to be the case with both the de Man followers and the traditionalists?

A: Yes. At a certain level of graduate training it's a little like boot camp, and there are attitudes and demeanors built into the situation. One of them in graduate programs in English involves this: "Oh there's nothing so darned special about Milton. We can wrassle that beast to the ground! There's nothing so darned special about Blake. We can figure him out and say he's not that interesting" (laughs). There's something of what one might call an undergraduate attitude of superiority over the texts being discussed. I believe that attitude dissipates at higher levels. And when the same professors go back to teaching undergraduates, they convey their love and enjoyment of the work. When they're teaching graduate students, however, it seems to be this hazing where we all have to agree that nothing is great. Everything needs to be defrauded; we need to prove to one another that we haven't been "fooled" by literature. It's very odd. I left one step ahead of a nervous breakdown.

Q: It only took a year?

A: Less than a year. I spent much of my second semester in bed reading Dickens. I still haven't read *Barnaby Rudge*, but I've read all the others. I read or reread all of his novels that semester, in bed, in my pj's. I didn't go to class.

Q: That sounds horribly depressing.

A: I had my own personal crisis under the covers (laughs). And on the day I decided to leave, I wrote a poem. Which is the first poem in my first book, "Landscape Poetry is a Dead Letter"—a reply to something a teacher had said dismissively about pastoral poetry.

Q: In the '80s you were an editor at *Vanity Fair*, *Premiere*, Bantam Books, and elsewhere. How has editing influenced your writing? Why did you stop?

A: Why did I stop? Better question is why did I start? When I left college, I was given very good advice by my beloved, wonderful, adored teacher, Robert Fitzgerald, the great translator and poet. He told me not to go to an MFA program; he said it would bore me to death. He told me to go to New York and work. I took his advice. I went and worked as a secretary at the *New York Review of Books* for two years and then went to graduate school, hated it, and went back to New York. First as a secretary at *Vanity Fair*. The magazine was being revived, so it was a start-up, and I was promoted from the editor-in-chief's secretary to an assistant editor to an editor, and then I kind of skipped around, editing at various glossy magazines. I was also starting to write book reviews, first for *Kirkus Review* and then for *The Nation*. Meanwhile, at the glossies, I wrote a lot of short pieces, captions, heads, and decks. It made me much more professional as a writer. It made me quick.

I really like editing. I had a great job at *Manhattan, inc.*, where I worked for a brilliant woman named Jane Amsterdam. But most of the time the magazine jobs were pretty puerile. You tried to do good work, but there really wasn't room. I was present during the big transition in the magazine business. I witnessed a change from a time when magazines expected to be able to support journalists, give them the financial backing of a magazine to get their jobs done—to a time of not giving them any help at all. The transition from the kind of ideal world where a magazine is present at the generation of stories to a less ideal world where a magazine is just reacting like every other medium to the world that's out there. Monthly magazines are hopeless at this anyway, because they can't be as fast as CNN news,; they can't respond with the same speed so they always end up behind the curve. So why not do something worthwhile instead? A magazine like the old *New Yorker* would actually underwrite journalists to embark on important work for a long period of time. They were trusting the writer and trusting the story. They made news. John Hersey's Hiroshima pieces, Rachel Carson's *Silent Spring*. They made the news; they weren't just reacting to it. That kind of ideal was still present when I first got into magazines. It had vanished by the time I left. The economics of the business had shifted so completely that nobody was thinking that way anymore at all. It was virtually all celebrity culture and publicity placements.

But I don't mean to imply that I took the high road myself. I've done my share of schlock. In 1992 I wrote an article called "My Life as a Blonde" for *Allure* magazine. I wrote about being a platinum blonde for a month. It was ridiculous. I was dragged uptown to this salon, dyed Jean Harlow-white-blonde, and had to write about it. I tried to be funny in the piece but felt like I had reached a kind of personal nadir. Then the *Allure* editors got mad at me because when I was asked to be a guest on

"Geraldo", I turned the TV show down—I thought I had been humiliated enough. It was grotesque. Right around then, thank God, the writer Caryl Phillips read my first book of poems and my novel and invited me to be the Visiting Writer at Amherst College. Before that, I had done a little spot teaching here and there, just trying to see if I liked it, but it was my first real teaching job, and it saved my life.

Q: Do you think you'll write another novel?

A: Oh yeah.

Q: Are you writing one now?

A: I wrote a second novel after *Pirate Jenny*. In fact, one of the great traumas of my adult life was not getting that novel published. I finished it in 1993 and tried to get it published for two years. Some people said that they liked it but it was too literary, and some people just hated it flat out (laughs). I decided that it was definitely too literary and perhaps hateful as well.

I'm working on another novel now.

Q: Do you not want to talk about it?

A: No. I'll finish it when I have time, which is never. My husband and I have a deal: We each get every other summer. So the summer before last I went to Yaddo for a month, and I started on this novel. I wrote a big part of it. But I haven't really gotten back to it and probably won't until I go to a colony this coming summer for a month. I hate being away from my son, but I have to be away from everybody to write prose.

Q: You mentioned once that John Ashbery's poem "The Skaters" changed your life. Can you elaborate?

A: It's one of the most extraordinary poems ever written. Like a great novel—it changes your life in the duration of reading it. Every time I read it, it changes my life again. I first read it in college, and I remember this magical sense not unlike the Elizabeth Bishop thing I described to you earlier. The sense that you could do so much in a poem. The poem is novelistic, it's cinematic, it's personal, it's lyrical, it expands and contracts and focuses, it's incredible. He does that in a lot of his long poems, but for some reason "The Skaters" remains my favorite. I'm attached to certain figures in the poems—the image of the skaters themselves, inscribing the ice with gestures, the way he plays with the night sky, the way, I believe, he's playing with images from Flemish painting, making a Brueghel-style winter landscape that he moves in and out of through the whole poem.

The poem is both inhabiting the landscape and seeing it from a distance.

Q: Whom do you consider to be your poet ancestors?

A: It's a pretty crowded tree. I think if Hopkins were alive and could read my poems and tell me that they were good, I'd probably be happier than anything else that could happen in my whole life. But the weird thing about writing is that I feel that I'm writing for him anyway. I just hope they don't make him sick, up there in heaven (laughs). I don't expect him to be pleased by them, but I hope they don't make him throw up. ✧

Henry James on Turgenev

The following first appeared in *Library of the World's Best Literature,*
edited by Charles Dudley Warner (New York: International Society, 1897).

There is perhaps no novelist of alien race who more naturally than Ivan
Turgenev inherits a niche in a Library for English readers; and this not
because of any advance or concession that in his peculiar artistic independence he ever made, or could dream of making, such readers, but
because it was one of the effects of his peculiar genius to give him, even
in his lifetime, a special place in the regard of foreign publics. His position is in this respect singular; for it is his Russian savor that as much as
anything has helped generally to domesticate him.

Born in 1818, at Orel in the heart of Russia, and dying in 1883, at
Bougival near Paris, he had spent in Germany and France the latter half
of his life; and had incurred in his own country in some degree the reprobation that is apt to attach to the absent—the penalty they pay for such
extension or such beguilement as they may have happened to find over
the border. He belonged to the class of large rural proprietors of land and
of serfs; and with his ample patrimony, offered one of the few examples
of literary labor achieved in high independence of the question of gain—
a character that he shares with his illustrious contemporary Tolstoy, who
is of a type in other respects so different. It may give us an idea of his primary
situation to imagine some large Virginian or Carolinian slaveholder, during
the first half of the century, inclining to 'Northern' views; and becoming
(though not predominantly under pressure of these, but rather by the
operation of an exquisite genius) the great American novelist—one of
the great novelists of the world. Born under a social and political order
sternly repressive, all Turgenev's deep instincts, all his moral passion,
placed him on the liberal side; with the consequence that early in life,
after a period spent at a German university, he found himself, through the
accident of a trifling public utterance, under such suspicion in high
places as to be sentenced to a term of tempered exile confinement to his
own estate. It was partly under these circumstances perhaps that he gathered material for the work from the appearance of which his reputation
dates—*A Sportsman's Sketches*, published in two volumes in 1852. This
admirable collection of impressions of homely country life, as the old
state of servitude had made it, is often spoken of as having borne to the
great decree of Alexander II the relation borne by Mrs. Beecher Stowe's
famous novel to the emancipation of the Southern slaves. Incontestably,
at any rate, Turgenev's rustic studies sounded, like *Uncle Tom's Cabin*, a
particular hour: with the difference, however, of not having at the time

produced an agitation—of having rather presented the case with an art too insidious for instant recognition, an art that stirred the depths more than the surface.

The author was designated promptly enough, at any rate, for such influence as might best be exercised at a distance: he travelled, he lived abroad; early in the sixties he was settled in Germany; he acquired property at Baden-Baden, and spent there the last years of the prosperous period—in the history of the place—of which the Franco-Prussian War was to mark the violent term. He cast in his lot after that event mainly with the victims of the lost cause; setting up a fresh home in Paris—near which city he had, on the Seine, a charming alternate residence—and passing in it, and in the country, save for brief revisitations, the remainder of his days. His friendships, his attachments, in the world of art and of letters, were numerous and distinguished; he never married; he produced, as the years went on, without precipitation or frequency; and these were the years during which his reputation gradually established itself as, according to the phrase, European—a phrase denoting in this case, perhaps, a public more alert in the United States even than elsewhere.

Tolstoy, his junior by ten years, had meanwhile come to fruition; though, as in fact happened, it was not till after Turgenev's death that the greater fame of *War and Peace* and of *Anna Karenina* began to be blown about the world. One of the last acts of the elder writer, performed on his deathbed, was to address to the other (from whom for a considerable term he had been estranged by circumstances needless to reproduce) an appeal to return to the exercise of the genius that Tolstoy had already so lamentably, so monstrously forsworn.

> I am on my death-bed; there is no possibility of my recovery. I write you expressly to tell you how happy I have been to be your contemporary, and to utter my last, my urgent prayer. Come back, my friend, to your literary labors. That gift came to you from the source from which all comes to us. Ah, how happy I should be could I think you would listen to my entreaty! My friend, great writer of our Russian land, respond to it, obey it!

These words, among the most touching surely ever addressed by one great spirit to another, throw an indirect light—perhaps I may even say a direct one—upon the nature and quality of Turgenev's artistic temperament; so much so that I regret being without opportunity, in this place, to gather such aid for a portrait of him as might be supplied by following out the unlikeness between the pair. It would be too easy to say that Tolstoy was, from the Russian point of view, for home consumption, and Turgenev for foreign: *War and Peace* has probably had more readers in Europe and America than *A House of Gentlefolk* or *On the Eve* or *Smoke*— a circumstance less detrimental than it may appear to my claim of our having, in the Western world, supremely adopted the author of the latter works. Turgenev is in a peculiar degree what I may call the novelists' novelist—an artistic influence extraordinarily valuable and ineradicably established. The perusal of Tolstoy—a wonderful mass of life—is an immense event, a kind of splendid accident, for each of us: his name represents nevertheless no such eternal spell of method, no such quiet irresistibility of presentation, as shines, close to us and lighting our possible steps, in that of his precursor. Tolstoy is a reflector as vast as a natural lake; a monster harnessed to his great subject—all human life!—as an elephant might be harnessed, for purposes of traction, not to a carriage, but to a coach-house. His own case is prodigious, but his example for others dire: disciples not elephantine he can only mislead and betray.

One by one, for thirty years, with a firm, deliberate hand, with intervals and patiences and waits, Turgenev pricked in his sharp outlines. His great external mark is probably his concision: an ideal he never threw over—it shines most perhaps even when he is least brief—and that he often applied with a rare felicity. He has masterpieces of a few pages; his perfect things are sometimes his least prolonged. He abounds in short tales, episodes clipped as by the scissors of Atropos; but for a direct translation of the whole we have still to wait—depending meanwhile upon the French and German versions, which have been, instead of the original text (thanks to the paucity among us of readers of Russian), the source of several published in English. For the novels and *A Sportsman's Sketches* we depend upon the nine volumes (1897) of Mrs. Garnett. We touch here upon the remarkable side, to our vision, of the writer's fortune—the anomaly of his having constrained to intimacy even those who are shut out from the enjoyment of his medium, for whom that question is positively prevented from existing. Putting aside extrinsic intimations, it is impossible to read him without the conviction of his being, in the vividness of his own tongue, of the strong type of those made to bring home to us the happy truth of the unity, in a generous talent, of material and form—of their being inevitable faces of the same medal; the type of those, in a word, whose example deals death to the perpetual clumsy assumption that subject and style are—aesthetically speaking, or in the living work—different and separable things. We are conscious, reading him in a language not his own, of not being reached by his personal tone, his individual accent.

It is a testimony therefore to the intensity of his presence, that so much of his particular charm does reach us; that the mask turned to us has, even without his expression, still so much beauty. It is the beauty (since we must try to formulate) of the finest presentation of the familiar. His vision is of the world of character and feeling, the world of the relations life throws up at every hour and on every spot; he deals little, on the whole, in the miracles of chance—the hours and spots over the edge of time and space; his air is that of the great central region of passion and motive, of the usual, the inevitable, the intimate—the intimate for weal or woe. No theme that he ever chooses but strikes us as full; yet with all have we the sense that their animation comes from within, and is not pinned to their backs like the pricking objects used of old in the horse-races of the Roman carnival, to make the animals run. Without a patch of 'plot' to draw blood, the story he mainly tells us, the situation he mainly gives, runs as if for dear life. His first book was practically full evidence of what, if we have to specify, is finest in him—the effect, for the commonest truth, of an exquisite envelope of poetry. In this medium of feeling—full, as it were, of all the echoes and shocks of the universal danger and need—everything in him goes on; the sense of fate and folly and pity and wonder and beauty. The tenderness, the humor, the variety of *A Sportsman's Sketches* revealed on the spot an observer with a rare imagination. These faculties had attached themselves, together, to small things and to great: to the misery, the simplicity, the piety, the patience, of the unemancipated peasant; to all the natural wonderful life of earth and air and winter and summer and field and forest; to queer apparitions of country neighbors, of strange local eccentrics; to old-world practices and superstitions; to secrets gathered and types disinterred and impressions absorbed in the long, close contacts with man and nature involved in the passionate pursuit of game. Magnificent in stature and original vigor, Turgenev, with his love of the chase, or rather perhaps of the inspiration he found in it, would have been the model of the mighty hunter, had not such an image been a little at variance with his natural mildness, the softness that often accompanies the sense of an extraordinary reach of limb and play of muscle. He was in person the model rather of the strong man at rest: massive and towering, with the voice of innocence and the smile almost of childhood. What seemed still more of a contradiction to so much of him, however, was that his work was all delicacy and fancy, penetration and compression.

If I add, in their order of succession, *Rudin, Fathers and Children, Spring Floods*, and *Virgin Soil*, to the three novels I have (also in their relation of time) named above, I shall have indicated the larger blocks of the compact monument, with a base resting deep and interstices well filled, into which that work disposes itself. The list of his minor productions is too long to draw out: I can only mention, as a few of the most striking—*A Correspondence, The Wayside Inn, The Brigadier, The Dog, The Jew, Visions, Mumu, Three Meetings, A First Love, The Forsaken, Assia, The Journal of a Superfluous Man, The Story of Lieutenant Yergunov, A King Lear of the Steppe*. The first place among his novels would be difficult to assign: general opinion probably hesitates between *A House of Gentlefolk* and *Fathers and Children*. My own predilection is great for the exquisite *On the Eve*; though I admit that in such a company it draws no supremacy from being exquisite. What is less contestable is that *Virgin Soil*— published shortly before his death, and the longest of his fictions—has, although full of beauty, a minor perfection.

Character, character expressed and exposed, is in all these things what we inveterately find. Turgenev's sense of it was the great light that artistically guided him; the simplest account of him is to say that the mere play of it constitutes in every case his sufficient drama. No one has had a closer vision, or a hand at once more ironic and more tender, for the individual figure. He sees it with its minutest signs and tricks—all its heredity of idiosyncrasies, all its particulars of weakness and strength, of ugliness and beauty, of oddity and charm; and yet it is of his essence that he sees it in the general flood of life, steeped in its relations and contacts, struggling or submerged, a hurried particle in the stream. This gives him, with his quiet method, his extraordinary breadth; dissociates his rare power to particularize from dryness or hardness, from any peril of caricature. He understands so much that we almost wonder he can express anything; and his expression is indeed wholly in absolute projection, in illustration, in giving of everything the unexplained and irresponsible specimen. He is of a spirit so human that we almost wonder at his control of his matter; of a pity so deep and so general that we almost wonder at his curiosity. The element of poetry in him is constant, and yet reality stares through it without the loss of a wrinkle. No one has more of that sign of the born novelist which resides in a respect unconditioned for the freedom and vitality, the absoluteness when summoned, of the creatures he invokes; or is more superior to the strange and second-rate policy of explaining or presenting them by reprobation or apology—of taking the short cuts and anticipating the emotions and judgments about them that should be left, at the best, to the perhaps not most intelligent reader. And yet his system, as it may summarily be called, of the mere particularized report, has a lucidity beyond the virtue of the cruder moralist.

If character, as I say, is what he gives us at every turn, I should speedily add that he offers it not in the least as a synonym, in our Western sense, of resolution and prosperity. It wears the form of the almost helpless detachment of the short-sighted individual soul; and the perfection of his exhibition of it is in truth too often but the intensity of what, for success, it just does not produce. What works in him most is the question of the will; and the most constant induction he suggests, bears upon the sad figure that principle seems mainly to make among his countrymen. He had seen—he suggests to us—its collapse in a thousand quarters; and the most general tragedy, to his view, is that of its desperate adventures and disasters, its inevitable abdication and defeat. But if the men, for the most part, let it go, it takes refuge in the other sex; many of the representatives of which, in his pages, are supremely strong—in wonderful addition, in various cases, to being otherwise admirable. This is true of such a number—the younger women, the girls, the 'heroines' in especial—that they form in themselves, on the ground of moral beauty, of the finest distinction of soul, one of the most striking groups the modern novel has given us. They are heroines to the letter, and of a heroism obscure and undecorated: it is almost they alone who have the energy to determine and to act. Elena, Lisa, Tatyana, Gemma, Marianna—we can write their names and call up their images, but I lack space to take them in turn. It is by a succession of the finest and tenderest touches that they live; and this, in all Turgenev's work, is the process by which he persuades and succeeds.

It was his own view of his main danger that he sacrificed too much to detail; was wanting in composition, in the gift that conduces to unity of impression. But no novelist is closer and more cumulative; in none does distinction spring from a quality of truth more independent of everything but the subject, but the idea itself. This idea, this subject, moreover—a spark kindled by the innermost friction of things—is always as interesting as an unopened telegram. The genial freedom—with its exquisite delicacy —of his approach to this 'innermost' world, the world of our finer consciousness, has in short a side that I can only describe and commemorate as nobly disinterested; a side that makes too many of his rivals appear to hold us in comparison by violent means, and introduce us in comparison to vulgar things. ✧

3rdbed·com

2004 Colorado Prize for Poetry

$1500 Honorarium & Publication

DEADLINE

Book-length manuscripts accepted from October 1, 2003, through the postmark deadline of January 15, 2004. The winning manuscript will be announced in May 2004 and published by the Center for Literary Publishing in the fall of 2004.

READING FEE

The $25 reading fee includes a subscription to *Colorado Review.*

GUIDELINES

Manuscripts may consist of previously published poems, but collections as a whole must be unpublished. There is no minimum or maximum page count. Please obtain complete guidelines by e-mailing us at creview@colostate.edu, visiting us on the Web at www.coloradoreview.com, or sending an SASE to the address below.

Colorado Prize for Poetry
Colorado Review
Center for Literary Publishing
Dept. of English
Colorado State University
Fort Collins, CO 80523
(970) 491-5449

David S. Allee   Kathleen Andersen   Ky Anderson   Robert Archambeau   Mary Jo Bang   Edward Bartok-Baratta   Joshua Beckman John Beer   Debbie Benson   Walead Beshty   Beth Block   Laure-Anne Bosselaar   Jenny Boully   Joe Brainard   Pam Brown   Rafael Campo Jennifer Chang   Anna Collette   Billy Collins   Shanna Compton   Kevin Cooley   Michael Costello   Jason Danzinger   Sarah Darpli   Cort Day   Connie Deanovich   Albert Flynn DeSilver   Geoffrey Detrani   Trane Devore   Ray

ART ESSAYS FICTION PHOTOGRAPHY POETRY

DiPalma   Sharon Dolin   Brady Dollarhide   Wei Dong   Mary Donnelly Denise Duhamel   Richard Dupont   Corwin Ericson   George J Farrah   MK Fancisco   Jay Gardner   Amy Gerstler   John Gossage   Arielle Greenberg Carl Gunhouse   Jane Hammond   Kristen Hanlon   Harrison Haynes   Lyn Hejinian   Steven A Heller   Alexander Heilner   Alex Heminway   Stephen Hilger   Shannon Holman   Henry Israeli   Shelley Jackson   Christopher

C R O W D

Kelty   Lisa Kereszi   Barbara Kruger   Christine Kuan   Debora Kuan   Susan Landers   John Latta   Brett Fletcher Lauer   David Dodd Lee   David Lehman Ben Lerner   Luljeta Lleshanaku   Timothy Liu   Joyelle McSweeney   Richard Meier   Lynn Melnick   Charlotte Mew   Toni Mirosevich   Matthew Monteith Nick Montfort   Malena Morling   Paul Muldoon   Ryan Murphy   Geoffrey G. O'Brien   Kathleen Ossip   Ron Padgett   Danielle Pafunda   Ethan Paquin Hyun-Doo Park   Christa Parravani   Chris Prentice   Richard Prince   David

487 UNION ST #3 BROOKLYN NY 11231

WWW.CROWDMAGAZINE.COM

Prete   Kathryn Rantala   Julie Reid   Andrew Rodgers   Andy Ryan   Mark Salerno   Maureen Seaton   Ravi Shankar   Steven Sherrill   Lori Shine   Amy Sillman   Sean Singer   Hugh Steinberg   AL Steiner   Virgil Suarez   Derek Stroup   Cole Swensen   James Tate   Matthew Thorburn   David Todd   Wells Tower   Laura Gail Tyler   Michael Vahranwald   Kara Walker   Clay Weiner Timothy Westmoreland   Susan Wheeler   Sam White   Marina Wilson   Ofer Wolberger   Rebecca Wolff   Matthew Zapruder   Rachel Zucker

Gettysburg
The Gettysburg Review

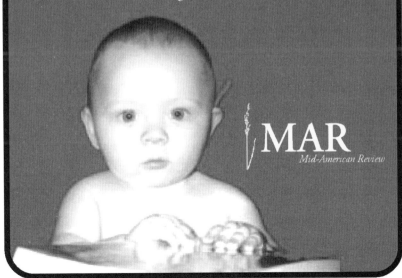

Have fun,

Be lucky.

Mississippi Review

For information write the Center for Writers, The University of Southern Mississippi,
Box 5144, Hattiesburg, MS 39406-5144 (AA/EOE/ADAI), Telephone 601-266-4321,
or E-mail rief@netdoor.com. Online at www.mississippireview.com

NOON

NOON

1369 MADISON AVENUE PMB 298 NEW YORK NEW YORK 10128-0711

SUBSCRIPTION $9 DOMESTIC AND $14 FOREIGN

www.opencity.org

Open City #17 cover painting by Stu Mead

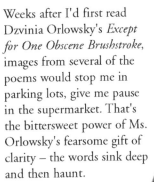

Weeks after I'd first read
Dzvinia Orlowsky's *Except
for One Obscene Brushstroke*,
images from several of the
poems would stop me in
parking lots, give me pause
in the supermarket. That's
the bittersweet power of Ms.
Orlowsky's fearsome gift of
clarity – the words sink deep
and then haunt.
        –Dennis Lehane

EXCEPT FOR ONE
Obscene Brushstroke

Carnegie Mellon University Press
c/o Cornell University Press Services
ISBN 0-88748-387-9
Paper $12.95
Credit Card Orders: **1-800-666-2211**

DZVINIA ORLOWSKY